SCRAP QUILT
secrets

6 Design Techniques for Knockout Results

Diane D. Knott

Text copyright © 2016 by Diane D. Knott
Photography and artwork copyright © 2016 by
C&T Publishing, Inc.

Publisher: Amy Marson
Creative Director: Gailen Runge
Editors: Lynn Koolish and Joanna Burgarino
Technical Editors: Ellen Pahl and Del Walker
Cover Designer: April Mostek
Book Designer: Christina Jarumay Fox
Production Coordinator: Freesia Pearson Blizard
Production Editor: Alice Mace Nakanishi
Illustrator: Aliza Shalit
Photo Assistant: Sarah Frost
Photography by Diane Pedersen, unless otherwise noted

Published by C&T Publishing, Inc., P.O. Box 1456,
Lafayette, CA 94549

All rights reserved. No part of this work covered by the copyright hereon may be used in any form or reproduced by any means—graphic, electronic, or mechanical, including photocopying, recording, taping, or information storage and retrieval systems—without written permission from the publisher. The copyrights on individual artworks are retained by the artists as noted in *Scrap Quilt Secrets*. These designs may be used to make items for personal use only and may not be used for the purpose of personal profit. Items created to benefit nonprofit groups, or that will be publicly displayed, must be conspicuously labeled with the following credit: Designs copyright © 2016 by Diane D. Knott from the book *Scrap Quilt Secrets* from C&T Publishing, Inc. Permission for all other purposes must be requested in writing from C&T Publishing, Inc.

Attention Copy Shops: Please note the following exception—publisher and author give permission to photocopy pages 17, 18, 33, 37, 47, 51, 65–67, 86, 87, 92, and 101–110 for personal use only.

Attention Teachers: C&T Publishing, Inc., encourages you to use this book as a text for teaching. Contact us at 800-284-1114 or ctpub.com for lesson plans and information about the C&T Creative Troupe.

We take great care to ensure that the information included in our products is accurate and presented in good faith, but no warranty is provided nor are results guaranteed. Having no control over the choices of materials or procedures used, neither the author nor C&T Publishing, Inc., shall have any liability to any person or entity with respect to any loss or damage caused directly or indirectly by the information contained in this book. For your convenience, we post an up-to-date listing of corrections on our website (ctpub.com). If a correction is not already noted, please contact our customer service department at ctinfo@ctpub.com or at P.O. Box 1456, Lafayette, CA 94549.

Trademark (™) and registered trademark (®) names are used throughout this book. Rather than use the symbols with every occurrence of a trademark or registered trademark name, we are using the names only in the editorial fashion and to the benefit of the owner, with no intention of infringement.

Library of Congress Cataloging-in-Publication Data
Knott, Diane D., 1966- author.
  Scrap quilt secrets : 6 design techniques for knockout results / Diane D. Knott.
     pages cm
  ISBN 978-1-61745-138-6 (soft cover)
  1. Patchwork--Patterns. 2. Quilting--Patterns. I. Title.
  TT835.K585 2016
  746.46'041--dc23
                              2015027783

Printed in China
10 9 8 7 6 5 4 3 2 1

contents

SPECIAL THANKS...4

INTRODUCTION...5

SCRAPS SECRETS...6
S Is for Style • C Is for Contrast
• R Is for Repetition • A Is for Accent
• P Is for Palette • S Is for Selvage

USING *Style*...8
  Citrus Squeeze...9
  Homespun Hearts...12
  Windblown Wishes...19

USING *Contrast*...24
  Tipsy Tac Toe...26
  Crazy Daisy...30
  Zephyr...34

USING *Repetition*...38
  Fusion...40
  Sawnee Shadows...44
  Paper Chain...48

USING *Accents*...52
  Four-Patch Plaid...53
  Detour...56
  Razzmatazz...60

USING *Palettes*...68
  Oh My Stars...70
  Vintage Village...76
  Peppermint Pie...80

USING *Selvages*...88
  Gift Baskets...89

QUILTMAKING BASICS...93
Supplies • Design Surface • Rotary Cutting
• Sewing • Pressing • Making Half-Square
Triangles • Making and Using Templates
• Appliqué • Quilt Finishing

BLANKS FOR COLORING...101

ABOUT THE AUTHOR...111

RESOURCES...111

Dedication

To my children, Kelly, David, and Danny, who make me feel like the luckiest mom in the world. Their laughter and joy fill our home (and my heart) with so much love.

To my husband, Bill, my best friend, who believes in me even when I forget to believe in myself. I'm so thankful that he is my partner in parenting, love, and life.

Special Thanks

So many people supported and encouraged me during the writing of this book. I could not have tackled a project this large without their help, advice, hugs, and kind words.

Mary Ruth McDonald has been my friend, confidant, and quilting companion for more than fifteen years. We have traveled far and wide together and laughed all the way, in spite of the chickens! I will always treasure every memory we have made together.

My quilting bee group generously offered me their time, opinions, and encouragement. Anne Roth, Darlene Johnson, Kathy Schmidt, Mary Ruth McDonald, and Patsy Eckman have been with me every step of the way. They are my mentors, friends, and stitching sisters. I am so blessed to have them in my life.

My guild friends have responded with so much enthusiasm to every project I have made. They make me feel supported and lift me up when I need it most, especially my sweet friend Martha Brach.

Betty Alonsious quilted many of the quilts in this book. It's easy to trust someone who is so talented and caring. She devoted her amazing skills and many hours to the quilts in this book. I am so grateful that she is my friend.

My husband, Bill, has taken over more than his share of parenting and household duties while I quilted and typed. He never failed to accommodate my crazy schedule, fix my laptop, or just bring me another cup of coffee. My children, Kelly, David, and Danny, inspire me with their passion, courage, and commitment every day. They never once complained about the undone laundry or the hours I spent locked in my sewing room. They also provided many distractions and much-needed perspective on a daily basis.

And finally, to the folks at C&T Publishing, who shared my vision and gave me the opportunity to turn a dream into reality, thank you.

Introduction

The question I hear most often while teaching workshops is, "How did you think of that?" People want to know, when I see a quilt and I re-create it with my own fabrics, how I got from the photo or quilt in front of me to the new version, which is often very different from the original inspiration. It's simple: I have a few steps I follow and a few secrets that I keep in mind.

First, I ask myself, What is it that I like most about this quilt? Is it the color, pattern, or fabric? Is it the overall style or feel of the quilt? Is it a certain detail or element? I make sure that my answers to these questions will be the same in the quilt I am making. By choosing the elements that I really like the best, I can be sure that those elements don't get lost in translation. What I love about the inspiration quilt will be the same thing I love in my quilt, even if the two quilts are very different in other ways. If I can pinpoint the specific elements that I like best about a quilt, I can make other choices I like better when selecting fabric, patterns, or quilting designs for my own quilt.

Second, I ask, How will this quilt be used? The answer determines many things. If it's going to be for a baby, it will need to be washable, durable, and safe for an infant. If the quilt is a wedding gift, I make sure it is the correct size for the newlyweds' bed (if unsure, a large throw size is always good). I will make it fit the wedding theme, use the colors in their new home, or feature something they love. I choose color combinations and style that are their taste, not mine. If it's a graduation quilt, school colors are always a good choice.

Third, I always remember to be realistic about my skill set. I know I cannot hand quilt a king-size quilt in a reasonable amount of time. On the other hand, I know that I have successfully quilted many king-size quilts on my sewing machine, and I love to hand quilt smaller projects. Also, I prefer hand appliqué to paper piecing, so I am more inclined to choose a pattern that uses appliqué. Better yet, I look for patterns in which the paper piecing can be easily changed to appliqué. By using my skills to their best advantage while being realistic about the quiltmaking process, I can achieve great results and enjoy the journey.

In the following pages I offer six secrets to making successful scraps quilts, but the most important thing is to follow your heart. Choose the fabrics and designs that inspire you—by knowing what you want and how to accomplish it, you can make the choices in the beginning that will give you a quilt you really love in the end. The secrets in this book are meant to expand your options, not limit them. I hope you find that each choice you make brings you one step closer to finishing the quilt of your dreams. Enjoy every stitch!

Diane

Scraps SECRETS

Everyone loves being let in on a secret! I have six secrets I want share with you about quilting with scraps. I'm sure there are more, but these basics are the foundation for using your entire fabric stash, even the tiniest scraps, to make quilts that truly represent your personality.

You bought all that fabric because you loved it (or because it was on a really good sale). You made quilts or other projects from it and now have small pieces you don't want to waste—a sign that you were born to be a scrap quilter. Now you just need to know how to use those scraps in ways that look good. Not every scrap needs to be added to the same quilt, unless you want it to. The decisions are entirely up to you; however, if you want a little help with the process, here are my six secrets to making scrap quilts. I've arranged the secrets into the acronym **SCRAPS** to make them easy to remember. Follow these six simple rules and you'll be well on your way to making scrap quilts that you will love.

S Is for Style

Style is so much more than just a description, such as folk, modern, traditional, primitive, and so on. It's about your personal twist on an idea. Do you love flowery pastels? Do you gravitate toward geometrics and bright colors? Are you drawn to homespun fabrics and plaids? All of these things can, and do, fit into more than one style. Remember, just because you see a quilt made in a particular style doesn't mean you can't change it. For example, you can change the style of a quilt from romantic to primitive by choosing different fabrics and perhaps adding some wool appliqué. Change a traditional-looking quilt to contemporary simply by choosing modern colors. Use homespun fabrics and historical blocks and settings for a vintage feel.

By choosing a style you like, you'll be well on your way to making a quilt that makes you happy, even without a trip to the fabric shop.

C Is for Contrast

Contrast is simply light versus dark—nothing more. But what about all those medium-value fabrics in your scrap bin? If you use those medium-value fabrics with light-value fabrics, they will appear dark. Similarly, if you pair those mediums with black or dark-value fabrics, they will appear light. It depends on what they are next to. Practice arranging fabrics in different combinations to see how contrast creates the design of the quilt more than any other single element.

Medium-value fabric next to light fabric looks dark.

Medium-value fabric next to dark fabric looks light.

R Is for Repetition

Repetition doesn't refer only to rows of repeating blocks. Repetition can also be seen in the shapes, fabrics, and colors used in a quilt. Using the same color in the same place in each block creates repetition, as does using the same background fabric in every block of an otherwise scrappy quilt. Repetition creates a sense of cohesion and allows different elements to look like they belong together. The consistency created by repetition keeps your scrappy design from getting out of control.

A Is for Accent

Think of an *accent color* as the scrap quilt's accessory. After all, a great outfit includes an accessory or two, so why shouldn't your quilt? One small but important color choice that stands out can make a whole quilt really special. The accent color needs to contrast with the main color and stand out to create a sparkle. Think of the accent color as the glue that holds all the other random colors in place, keeping the design from getting scrambled up too much. This is the perfect time to use that favorite fabric you've been saving!

P Is for Palette

Different color combinations will create entirely different quilts, even when made from the same blocks. Using a *color palette* to limit the colors in your scrap quilt provides a theme for the quilt and helps you eliminate colors that don't work. Setting limits such as *no white* or *only muted colors* can lend a vintage look to a quilt. Using a pastel palette without any primary colors gives your quilt a soft, romantic look. If you are making a scrap quilt for the man in your life, you might choose a darker, more subdued palette.

S Is for Selvages

Selvages are the lengthwise, tightly woven edges of the fabric as it comes off the bolt. Selvages are typically cut away and discarded before using the fabric, but they can be a bonus for scrap quilters who don't like to throw away any part of their fabric. It's easy enough to toss them all into a basket or bin and save them for later. The variety of prints and styles makes a quilt more interesting and adds a punch of color.

Accent fabric stands out among scraps.

Selvages

SCRAPS SECRETS

USING *Style*

What is it about a quilt that makes you gasp? Which quilts do you find yourself noticing the most? Are you a fan of soft pastels and blended designs? Are you always looking for that bright pop of color? Are you staring at your Pinterest boards and realizing that all of your quilts have black in them? Does patchwork that uses fussy-cut fabrics make you smile? Do folk or primitive patterns speak to you?

The quilts you love and the quilts you make say so much about your personal quilting style. None of us is strictly defined by our style choices, but determining what look pleases you most will help you to stay focused and make quilts you truly love.

CITRUS SQUEEZE

Pieced and quilted by Diane D. Knott

Finished quilt: 48″ × 60″

Finished block: 12″ × 12″

SKILL LEVEL: EASY

A quick and easy design, this quilt is perfect for gift giving. These bright colors make a fun baby quilt, but it would also be sweet in pinks or blues. Add a few more blocks and rows to make it big enough for a child's bed.

MATERIALS

- **Scraps in red, pink, orange, and yellow:** 2½ yards total
- **Solid white:** 1 yard
- **Backing:** 3¼ yards
- **Binding:** ½ yard
- **Batting:** 56˝ × 68˝

Share the Fun

If you need a wider variety of fabrics for your scrap quilt, organize an exchange with a group of friends. Be specific about what colors or styles you would like. Exchanges are a great way to add diversity to your fabrics and have fun at the same time.

CUTTING

All measurements include ¼˝-wide seam allowances.

Scraps
- Cut 180 rectangles 2½˝ × 3½˝.
- Cut 45 rectangles 4½˝ × 6½˝.

Solid white
- Cut 2 strips 12½˝ × width of fabric; subcut 15 strips 4½˝ × 12½˝.

Binding
- Cut 6 strips 2˝ × width of fabric.

Block Assembly

Refer to Quiltmaking Basics (page 93) as needed.

1. Sew together 6 rectangles 2½˝ × 3½˝ along the 3½˝ edges. Make 30 units. Don't press the seams yet.

2. Arrange the units from Step 1 in pairs; then press the seams in the top row to the right and in the bottom row to the left so that they will nest to reduce bulk. Sew the rectangle units together, matching the seams. Make 15 small rectangle units.

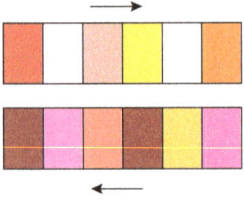

Press seams.

Make 15.

3. Sew together 3 rectangles 4½˝ × 6½˝. Make 15 large rectangle units. Don't press the seams yet.

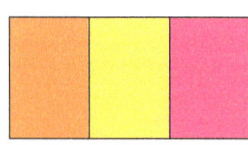

Make 15.

4. Arrange a unit from Step 3 together with a unit from Step 2 and then press the seams in the Step 3 unit so that they will nest. Sew the small rectangle unit to the large rectangle unit to make a block. Press all the seams toward the large rectangles. Make 15 blocks.

Block assembly—make 15.

Quilt Assembly

1. Sew a sashing strip to the right side of 9 blocks and to the left side of 6 blocks. Press the seams toward the sashing.

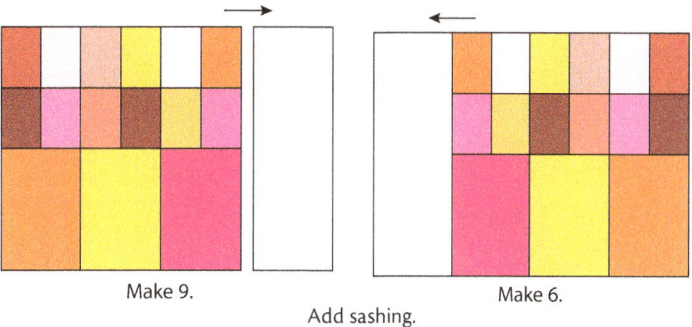

Make 9. Add sashing. Make 6.

2. Sew the blocks into 5 rows of 3 blocks, as shown in the quilt assembly diagram (below). Press the seams toward the sashing.

3. Sew the rows together. Press the seams in one direction.

4. Layer the quilt top, batting, and backing. Baste, quilt as desired, and bind. Refer to Quilt Finishing (page 98) for additional details.

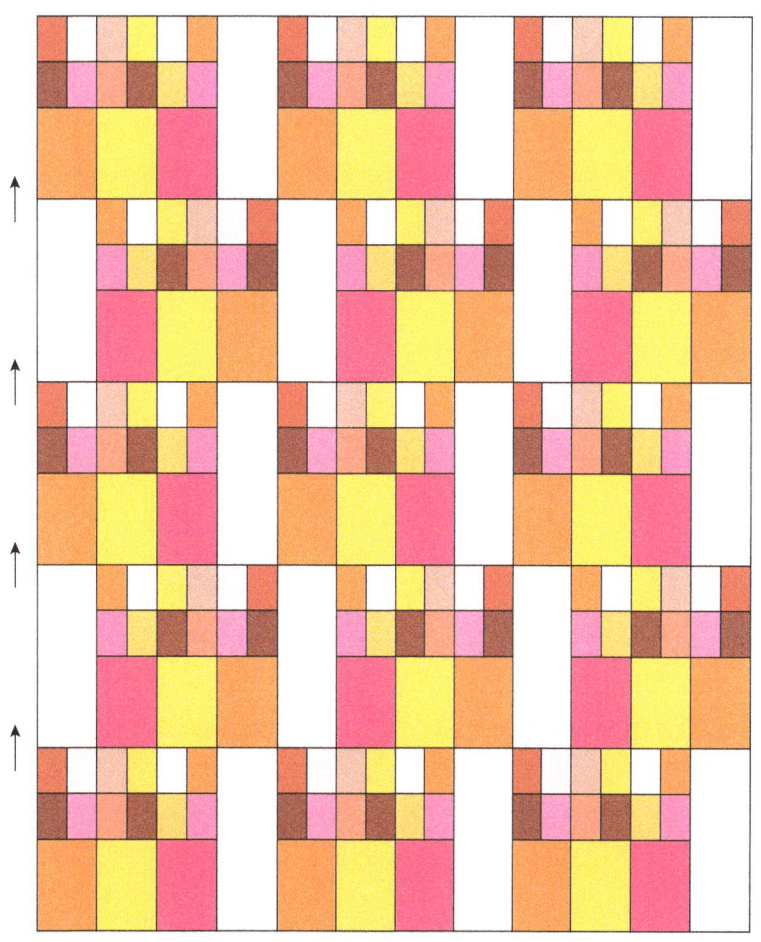

Quilt assembly

Secrets for a Modern Look

* Choose clear colors and crisp prints.

* Enlarge blocks, eliminate pieces, or choose basic patchwork for a bold look.

* Add solid fabrics or a white background to give scraps an updated image.

* Choose a simple quilting design.

HOMESPUN HEARTS

Pieced and quilted by Diane D. Knott

Finished quilt: 48″ × 54″

Finished blocks: 12″ × 18″, 3″ × 3″, and 6″ × 6″

SKILL LEVEL: MODERATE

Stars, hearts, a charming house, and an abundance of scraps work together to create this homespun treasure. All your scraps are candidates for this quilt, although it's especially appropriate for plaids, small-scale florals, and reproduction prints. It could be made in any fabrics, from batiks to modern prints and solids, to give it a different look.

MATERIALS

- **Red polka dot:** 1 fat quarter for center block
- **Dark green:** 4" × 13" piece for center block
- **Green plaid:** ⅓ yard for sashing
- **Blue scraps:** ⅓ yard total for half-square triangles
- **Brown scraps:** 1 yard total for half-square triangles and outer border
- **Cheddar fabric:** ⅓ yard for sashing
- **Scraps in blue, brown, red, cream, and gold:** 2¾ yards total for blocks
- **Red felted wool:** 4" × 12" piece
- **Green felted wool:** 3" × 8" piece
- **Gold felted wool:** 2½" × 3" piece
- **Rickrack:** ½ yard, ⅞" wide
- **Backing:** 3¼ yards
- **Binding:** ½ yard
- **Batting:** 56" × 62"
- **Freezer paper**

CUTTING

All measurements include ¼"-wide seam allowances.

Red polka dot
- Cut 1 rectangle 12½" × 15½".

Blue
- Cut 12 squares 4¼" × 4¼".

Dark green
- Cut 1 rectangle 3½" × 12½".

Green plaid
- Cut 2 strips 2" × 24½".
- Cut 2 strips 2" × 21½".

Cheddar
- Cut 2 strips 2" × 33½".
- Cut 2 strips 2" × 30½".

Brown
- Cut 12 squares 4¼" × 4¼".
- Cut 4 squares 3½" × 3½".
- Cut 30 rectangles 3½" × 6½".

Blue, brown, red, and cream scraps
- Cut 144 squares 2" × 2".
- Cut 26 matching sets of the following:

    1 square 3½" × 3½" and 8 squares 2" × 2"

    4 squares 2" × 2" and 4 rectangles 2" × 3½"

Binding
- Cut 6 strips 2" × width of fabric.

Secrets for Making Folk Art Fun

* Use shapes that are wonky or asymmetrical.
* Choose plaids, stripes, and homespun fabrics.
* Add wool, rickrack, or thread embellishments.
* Hand quilt with big stitches.
* Keep it simple.
* Never take it too seriously.

Center Block

Refer to Quiltmaking Basics (page 93) as needed.

1. Refer to Making and Using Templates (page 96) to make templates using the appliqué patterns (pages 17 and 18).

2. Refer to Appliqué (page 96) or use your favorite method to prepare the shapes. Cut the hearts, leaves, and star from wool and the remaining appliqués from the scraps of red, cream, brown, and gold.

3. Arrange the rickrack and appliqué shapes on the red polka dot 12½˝ × 15½˝ rectangle. Fuse or stitch them in place. Press the block from the wrong side.

4. Sew the dark green 3½˝ × 12½˝ rectangle to the bottom of the appliqué block. Press the seam toward the green fabric.

Center block—make 1.

Personalize Your Quilt

Change the colors of the house to match your own home. Add or subtract hearts according to how many people are in your family. Add pets, numbers, or dates that are meaningful to you and your loved ones.

Triangle Border

1. Make 24 half-square triangles (page 95) from the blue and brown 4¼˝ squares. Trim the units to 3½˝ × 3½˝.

2. Sew 6 half-square triangles into a row with the blue next to blue and brown next to brown. Press the seams open. Make 4 rows.

3. Sew 2 rows to the left and right sides of the center block. Press the seams toward the center block.

4. Sew 2 rows to the top and bottom of the center block as shown. Press the seams toward the center block.

Triangle border

Green Sashing

1. Sew the green 2˝ × 24½˝ strips to the left and right sides of the quilt center. Press the seams toward the strips.

2. Sew the green 2˝ × 21½˝ strips to the top and bottom of the quilt center. Press the seams toward the strips.

Four-Patch Border

1. Sew 4 of the 2″ × 2″ squares together in pairs. Press the seams in opposite directions. Sew the units together to make a four-patch. Pinwheel-press the seams (page 94). Make 36 blocks.

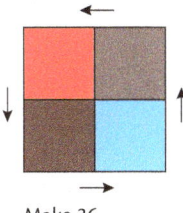

Make 36.

2. Sew 9 Four-Patch blocks together to make a border. Press the seams in one direction. Make 4 borders.

3. Sew a border to the left and right sides of the quilt. Press the seams toward the sashing.

4. Sew a border to the top and bottom of the quilt. Press the seams toward the sashing.

Add Four-Patch border.

Cheddar Sashing

1. Sew the cheddar 2″ × 33½″ strips to the left and right sides of the quilt. Press the seams toward the sashing.

2. Sew the cheddar 2″ × 30½″ strips to the top and bottom of the quilt. Press the seams toward the sashing.

Star Border

1. For each star block, choose a 3½″ × 3½″ square and 8 matching 2″ × 2″ squares for the star points. Choose a matching set of 4 squares, 2″ × 2″, and 4 rectangles, 2″ × 3½″, for the background.

2. Draw a diagonal line from corner to corner on the wrong side of the 2″ star squares. Place a square on a background rectangle, right sides together, and sew on the drawn line. Trim the excess fabric, leaving a ¼″ seam allowance. Press the seams away from the rectangle. Repeat on the other end of the rectangle as shown to make a flying geese unit for the star points. Make 4.

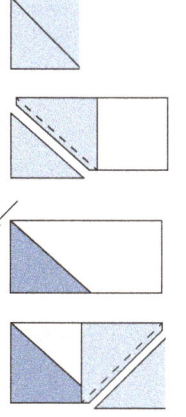

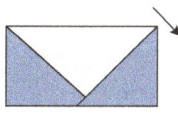

Make 4.

HOMESPUN HEARTS 15

3. Sew a flying geese unit to opposite sides of the 3½″ square. Press the seams toward the square. Sew a background 2″ square to each end of 2 flying geese units. Press the seams toward the squares.

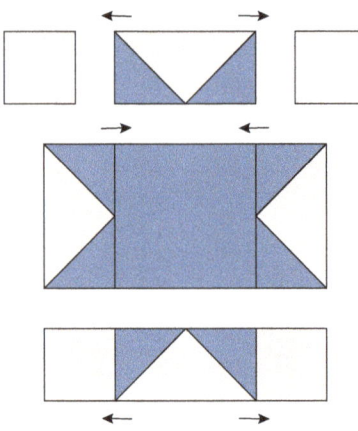

4. Sew the rows together. Press the seams toward the center row.

Star block assembly—make 26.

5. Sew 6 Star blocks together into a row. Make 2 rows for the side borders. Sew 7 Star blocks into a row for the top and bottom borders. Make 2 rows. Press the seams in one direction.

6. Sew the rows of 6 Star blocks onto the left and right sides of the quilt. Press the seams toward the sashing.

Sew the rows of 7 Star blocks onto the top and bottom of the quilt. Press the seams toward the sashing.

Outer Border

1. Sew 6 brown 3½″ × 6½″ rectangles together end to end. Sew a brown 3½″ × 3½″ square onto each end of the strip. Press the seams in one direction. Make 2 rows. Sew 9 brown 3½″ × 6½″ rectangles together in the same manner. Make 2 rows.

Make 2 of each.

2. Sew the borders with squares to the top and bottom of the quilt. Press the seams toward the border.

3. Sew the borders without squares to the left and right sides of the quilt. Press the seams toward the border.

Quilt Assembly

Layer the quilt top, batting, and backing. Baste, quilt as desired, and bind. Refer to Quilt Finishing (page 98) for additional details.

Quilt assembly

16 SCRAP QUILT SECRETS

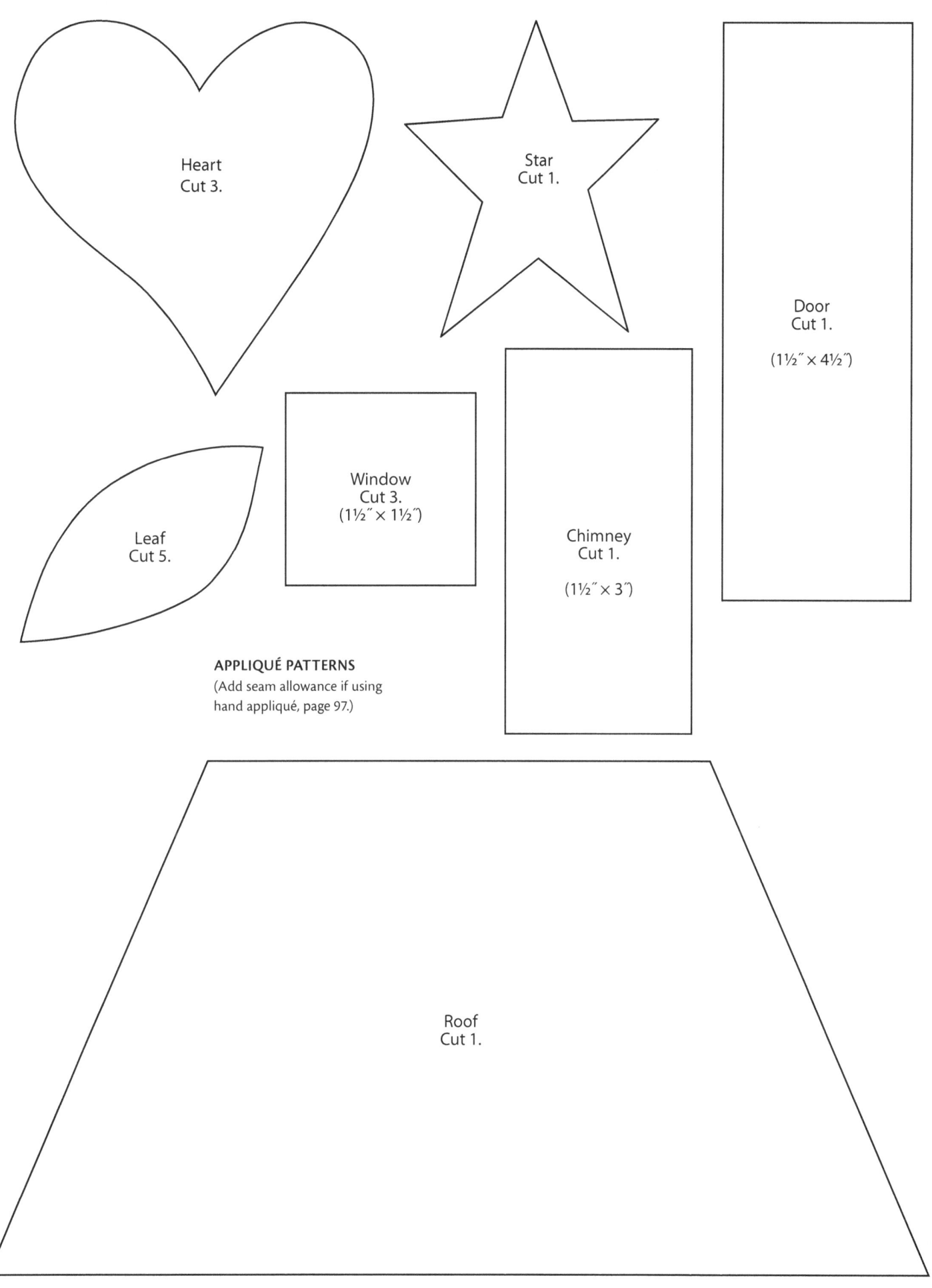

APPLIQUÉ PATTERNS
(Add seam allowance if using hand appliqué, page 97.)

HOMESPUN HEARTS

House
Cut 1.

(6″ × 8″)

APPLIQUÉ PATTERNS
(Add seam allowance if using hand appliqué, page 97.)

WINDBLOWN WISHES

Pieced and quilted by Diane D. Knott

Finished quilt: 61½" × 85½"

Finished block: 10½" × 10½"

SKILL LEVEL: MODERATE

This quilt contains the basic patchwork elements of squares and triangles, and features a traditional setting with sashing. Imagine, for a moment, how striking it would be made from patriotic fabrics. Or consider using 1930s fabrics and only half as many blocks for a baby quilt. The traditional colors, piecing, and setting make this design timeless.

MATERIALS

- **Red scraps:** 2 yards total
- **Black scraps:** ½ yard total
- **Green scraps:** ½ yard total
- **Tan scraps:** 3 yards total
- **Gold fabric:** ⅓ yard
- **Green border fabric:** ½ yard
- **Tan border fabric:** ½ yard
- **Red border fabric:** 2¼ yards
- **Backing:** 5¼ yards
- **Binding:** ⅔ yard
- **Batting:** 70″ × 94″

CUTTING

All measurements include ¼″-wide seam allowances.

Red scraps
- Cut 16 strips 2″ × 13″.
- Cut 76 squares 2″ × 2″.
- Cut 240 squares* 2¾″ × 2¾″.

Black scraps
- Cut 16 strips 2″ × 13″.

Green scraps
- Cut 16 strips 2″ × 13″.

Tan scraps
- Cut 48 strips 2″ × 13″.
- Cut 38 strips 2″ × 8″.
- Cut 111 squares 2″ × 2″.
- Cut 240 squares* 2¾″ × 2¾″.

Gold fabric
- Cut 4 strips 2″ × 13″.

Green border
- Cut 7 strips 2″ × width of fabric.

Tan border
- Cut 7 strips 2″ × width of fabric.

Red border
- Cut 2 strips 5″ × 77″.
- Cut 2 strips 5″ × 62″.

Binding
- Cut 8 strips 2″ × width of fabric.

* If you have a 45° triangle ruler, you can cut triangles from layered 2″-wide strips. See Using Strips (page 95).

Block Assembly

Refer to Quiltmaking Basics (page 93) as needed.

1. Sew together 2 green, 2 tan, and 1 red 2″ × 13″ strips as shown to make a strip set. Press the seams away from the tan strips. Make 8 strip sets. Crosscut each strip set into 6 segments 2″ wide. Cut 48 total. These will be rows 1 and 5 of the block.

Make 8 strip sets; cut 48 segments.

2. Sew 3 tan and 2 black 2″ × 13″ strips together as shown to make a strip set. Press the seams away from the tan strips. Make 8 strip sets. Crosscut each strip set into 6 segments 2″ wide. Cut 48 total. These will be rows 2 and 4 of the block.

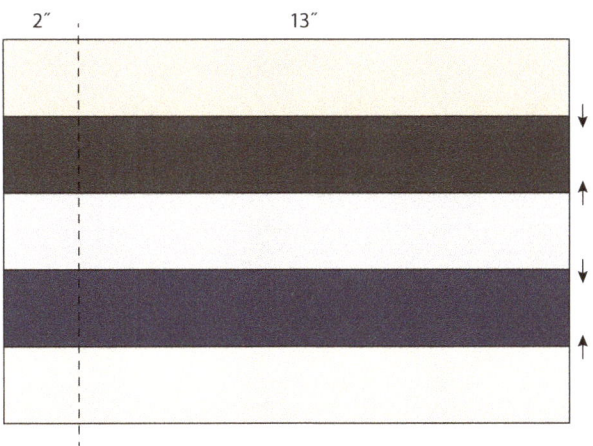

Make 8 strip sets; cut 48 segments.

3. Sew together 2 red, 2 tan, and 1 gold 2″ × 13″ strips as shown to make a strip set. Press the seams away from the tan strips. Make 4 strip sets. Crosscut each strip set into 6 segments 2″ wide. Cut 24 total. These will be row 3 of the block.

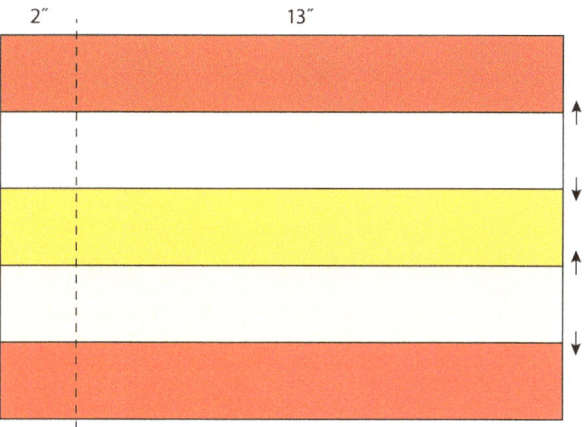

Make 4 strip sets; cut 24 segments.

4. Arrange the segments as shown and sew the rows together. Press the seams open. Make 24.

Make 24.

5. Make 480 half-square triangle units (page 95) using the 2¾″ squares of red and tan. Trim to 2″ × 2″.

WINDBLOWN WISHES 21

6. Sew the half-square triangles units into rows of 5. Make 96 rows.

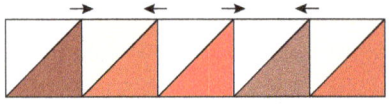

Make 96.

7. Sew a tan 2″ × 2″ square onto each end of 48 of the rows from Step 6.

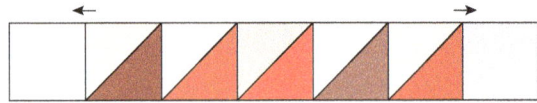

Add squares to 48 rows.

8. Sew a half-square triangle row to opposite sides of each checkerboard center, taking care to line up the seams. Press the seams away from the triangles. Sew a half-square triangle row with tan squares to the remaining sides of each block. Press the seams away from the triangles. The blocks should measure 11″ × 11″.

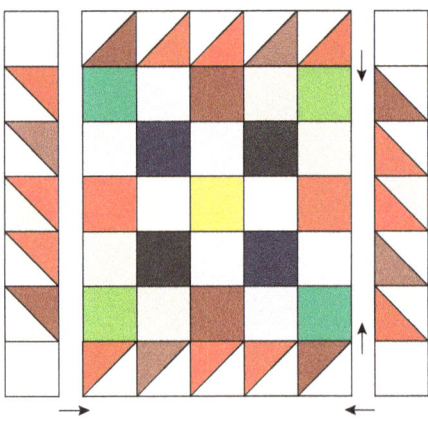

Block assembly—make 24.

Sashing Assembly

Sew a red 2″ × 2″ square onto each end of the 38 tan 2″ × 8″ sashing strips. Press the seams toward the red squares.

Sashing—make 38.

tip

Fast and Fun!

Make a table runner by simply sewing one row of blocks. Add sashing and a border, or just a binding.

22 SCRAP QUILT SECRETS

Quilt Assembly

1. Arrange the blocks in 6 rows of 4 blocks each, adding the sashing strips and 2″ tan squares. Sew the rows of blocks and sashing together and sew the sashing and sashing squares together. Press the seams toward the sashing. The quilt center should measure 47″ × 71″.

2. Sew the 7 green border strips end to end. Cut 2 strips 71″ long. Sew them to the left and right sides of the quilt top. Press the seams toward the borders.

3. Cut 2 green border strips 50″ long. Sew them to the top and bottom of the quilt top. Press the seams toward the borders.

4. Sew the 7 tan border strips end to end. Cut 2 strips 74″ long. Sew them to the left and right sides of the quilt top. Press the seams toward the borders.

5. Cut 2 tan border strips 53″ long. Sew them to the top and bottom of the quilt top. Press the seams toward the borders.

6. Sew the red 77″ border strips to the left and right sides of the quilt top. Press the seams toward the borders.

7. Sew the red 62″ border strips to the top and bottom of the quilt. Press the seams toward the borders.

8. Layer the quilt top, batting, and backing. Baste, quilt as desired, and bind. Refer to Quilt Finishing (page 98) for additional details.

Quilt assembly

Secrets for Timeless Tradition

* *Use classic colors and prints.*
* *Study vintage quilts for color combinations.*
* *Mix traditional blocks with traditional settings in a variety of ways to find your favorites.*
* *Consider a classic quilting design such as Baptist fan, clamshells, or a simple grid.*

WINDBLOWN WISHES

USING *Contrast*

High Contrast versus Low Contrast

A fabric that looks medium by itself can look dark next to a light fabric and light next to a dark fabric. It all depends on what it's snuggling up next to. Get crisp distinction between blocks by paying special attention to contrast. Likewise, you can create a blended look by using similar values of color next to each other.

Contrast is about creating clear dividing lines between different design elements or making them blend together. High contrast will give sharp definition to the shapes of the pieces in your quilt; low contrast will look blended or create smooth transitions from one piece to another. Contrast is much more important than color. My favorite scrap quilts are built around the concept of contrast. Choosing a few colors from your scraps and dividing the fabrics into lights and darks creates magic!

High contrast in *Tipsy Tac Toe* (page 26)—each block piece is distinct.

Low contrast in *Tipsy Tac Toe*—block pieces blend together.

Value

Value is simply how light or how dark a fabric appears. A good way to determine value, if it's not obvious, is to snap a photo of your fabrics lined up together. Looking at the photo makes it easier to distinguish lights from darks. Also, converting the photo to black and white will really show which fabrics fall into the light category and which ones fall into the dark category.

Large-Scale Prints

Large-scale prints can be tricky. Some portions of the fabric will read dark and others will read light. If you are cutting these up into smaller pieces or strips, you might need to divide them based on the pieces after they have been cut.

Are fabrics in order by value?

Large-scale print has dark areas and light areas.

Black-and-white photos help determine value.

TIPSY TAC TOE

Pieced by Diane D. Knott and quilted by Betty Alonsious

Finished quilt: 66″ × 66″

Finished block: 6″ × 6″

SKILL LEVEL: EASY

This quilt comprises two very simple blocks. The blocks are set on point in the quilt center and are repeated again in the border in a straight setting. Choosing fabrics with high contrast (very light and very dark) for the blocks in the quilt center and less contrast (medium fabrics) for the border blocks will make the center of the quilt appear to glow.

MATERIALS

- **Black scraps:** 3¼ yards total
- **White scraps:** 2¾ yards total
- **Backing:** 4¼ yards
- **Binding:** ⅝ yard
- **Batting:** 74″ × 74″

CUTTING

All measurements include ¼″-wide seam allowances.

Black scraps
- Cut 56 matching sets of 4 squares 2½″ × 2½″.
- Cut 56 squares 2½″ × 2½″.
- Cut 45 matching sets of 2 rectangles 2½″ × 6½″ and 2 squares 2½″ × 2½″.
- Cut 14 strips* 2″ × 18″.

* These pieces are for the inner border and should be solids or tone-on-tone prints.

White scraps
- Cut 56 matching sets of 4 squares 2½″ × 2½″ for X blocks.
- Cut 45 matching sets of 5 squares 2½″ × 2½″ for O blocks.
- Cut 5 squares 10″ × 10″ for side setting triangles; cut each square in quarters diagonally.
- Cut 2 squares 5½″ × 5½″ for corner triangles; cut each square in half diagonally.

Binding
- Cut 7 strips 2″ × width of fabric.

X Block Assembly

Refer to Quiltmaking Basics (page 93) as needed.

1. Arrange 4 matching black 2½″ × 2½″ squares, 1 different black square, and 4 matching white 2½″ × 2½″ squares in 3 rows as shown to make a 9-patch block. Sew the squares into rows.

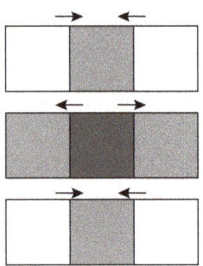

2. Sew the rows together. Press the seams as indicated by the arrows. The block should measure 6½″ × 6½″. Repeat to make 56 blocks.

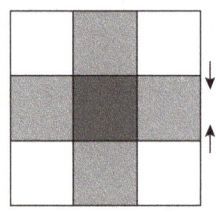

X block—make 56.

 tip

Chain Piecing

Chain piecing is a great way to save time and thread, as well as stay organized. Feed fabric pieces into the sewing machine one after another without clipping the thread in between. Clip the threads to separate the chain before pressing.

O Block Assembly

1. Choose 5 matching white 2½″ × 2½″ squares, a set of 2 matching black 2½″ × 2½″ squares, and 2 black 2½″ × 6½″ rectangles. Mark a diagonal line from corner to corner on the wrong side of 4 of the white squares.

2. Place a marked white square on each end of a black rectangle with right sides together. Sew on the drawn line, trim the seam allowances, and press toward the corners. Repeat with the second rectangle.

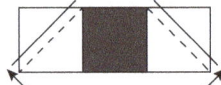 

3. Arrange the Step 2 units and the 3 squares as shown. Sew the squares together to create the middle row. Press the seams as indicated by the arrows. Sew the 3 rows together and press the seams according to the arrows. The block should measure 6½″ × 6½″. Repeat the steps to make 45 blocks.

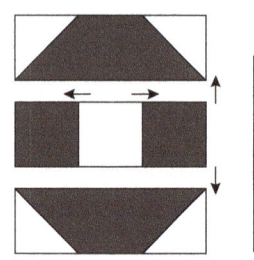 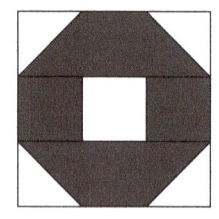

O block assembly—make 45.

Border Assembly

1. Sew the black 2″ × 18″ strips together, end to end. Cut 2 strips 51½″ and cut 2 strips 54½″ to make the inner borders.

2. Sew 9 blocks together for the left and right side borders, beginning and ending with X blocks. Sew 11 blocks together for the top and bottom borders, beginning and ending with O blocks. Press the seams toward the X blocks.

Quilt Assembly

1. Arrange the blocks in rows according to the quilt assembly diagram (below). Sew the blocks into diagonal rows, adding a setting triangle to the ends of each row as shown. Press the seams toward the X blocks.

2. Sew the rows together. Press the seams in one direction. Trim the edges and square up the corners so that the quilt center measures 51½" × 51½".

3. Sew the black 2" × 51½" borders to the left and right sides of the quilt. Press the seams toward the borders. Sew the 2" × 54½" borders to the top and bottom. Press the seams toward the borders.

4. Sew the 9-block outer borders to the left and right sides of the quilt. Press the seams toward the black border. Sew the 11-block borders to the top and bottom. Press the seams toward the black border.

5. Layer the quilt top, batting, and backing. Baste, quilt as desired, and bind. Refer to Quilt Finishing (page 98) for additional details.

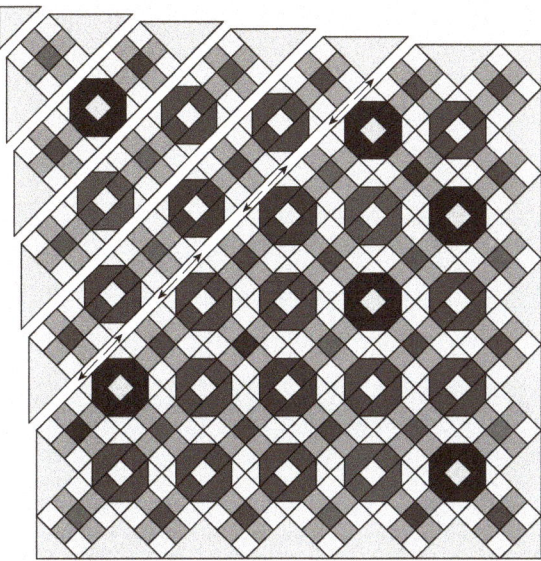

Quilt assembly

TIPSY TAC TOE 29

CRAZY DAISY

Pieced and quilted by Diane D. Knott

Finished quilt: 80″ × 80″
Finished block: 16″ × 16″

SKILL LEVEL: EASY

Always a fan of simple half-square triangles, I wanted to see what would happen if I made lots of them and added some appliqué. It needed to be fun and easy because my scraps were bright and playful. I paid no attention to contrast, or where the lights and darks landed within the blocks; I just let the fabrics arrange themselves. This quilt began with leftovers from six different fabric bundles, and I added more fabrics from my scrap basket.

MATERIALS

- **Scraps:** 6¾ yards total for blocks
- **Scraps:** ½ yard total for appliqué
- **Appliqué background:** 1½ yards
- **Backing:** 7⅓ yards
- **Binding:** ¾ yard
- **Batting:** 88″ × 88″
- **Freezer paper**

Mix and Match

Mix a set of precut fabrics in with your scraps. A set of precut fat quarters, strips, or squares is a great starting point for a scrap quilt. Be sure to add prints and colors that will not only blend in but add variety as well.

CUTTING

Make templates for the flowers, circles, stems, and leaves, using the patterns (page 33) and referring to Making and Using Templates (page 96). All measurements include ¼″-wide seam allowances.

Scraps for blocks

- Cut 320 squares* 5¼″ × 5¼″.

*If you have a 45° triangle ruler, you can cut triangles from layered 4½″-wide strips. See Using Strips (page 95).

Scraps for appliqué

- Cut 24 flowers.
- Cut 24 flower centers.
- Cut 24 stems.
- Cut 24 leaves.
- Cut 24 leaves reversed.

Appliqué background

- Cut 2 strips 8½″ × 32½″.
- Cut 2 strips 8½″ × 48½″.

Binding

- Cut 9 strips 2″ × width of fabric.

Block Assembly

Refer to Quiltmaking Basics (page 93) as needed.

1. Make 320 half-square triangles (page 95) using the 5¼″ squares. Trim the units to 4½″ × 4½″.

2. Sew 16 half-square triangles into 4 rows of 4 half-square triangles each as shown. Press the seams in opposing directions. Join the rows to make the 16-Patch block and press the seam in one direction. Repeat to make 20 blocks.

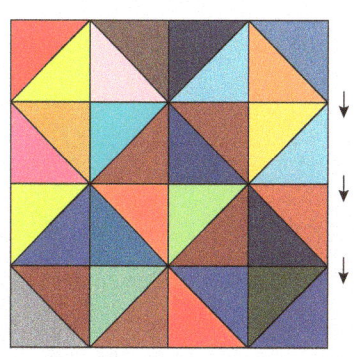

Make 20.

Appliqué

Use your favorite appliqué method, or refer to Appliqué (page 96).

1. Fold the background strips in half and press to mark the center of the borders.

2. Position the flowers, stems, and leaves onto the borders, centering the first stem, flower, and leaves on the creased line. Measure 6″ away on either side and add the next flower. Pin or fuse in place and stitch the appliqués by hand or machine. Place each flower 6″ away and alternate tall and short flowers by rotating the flower and changing its placement on the stem. Position the leaves lower on the stem for short flowers.

Top/bottom border appliqué placement

Side border appliqué placement

Quilt Assembly

1. Sew 4 blocks together to make the 32½″ × 32½″ center.

2. Sew the 2 borders that measure 8½″ × 32½″ to the top and bottom of the center section. Press the seams toward the border.

3. Sew the 2 borders 8½″ × 48½″ to the left and right sides of the quilt. Press the seams toward the borders.

4. Sew the remaining blocks into 2 rows of 3 and 2 rows of 5.

5. Sew the rows of 3 to the top and bottom of the quilt. Press the seams toward the appliquéd borders.

6. Sew the rows of 5 to the left and right sides of the quilt. Press the seams toward the appliquéd borders.

7. Layer the quilt top, batting, and backing. Baste, quilt as desired, and bind. Refer to Quilt Finishing (page 98) for additional details.

Quilt assembly

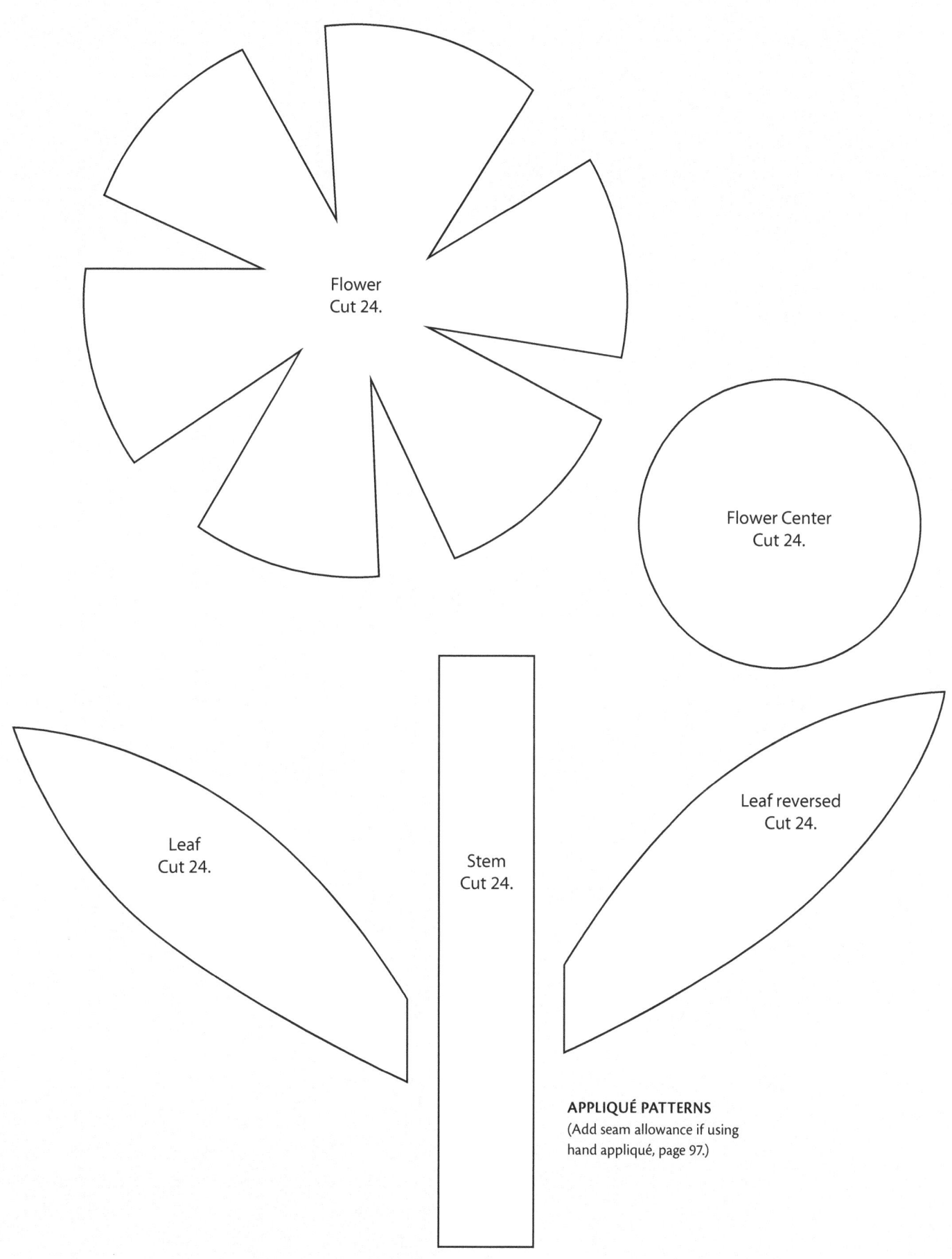

ZEPHYR

Pieced and quilted by Diane D. Knott

Finished quilt: 71″ × 81″

Finished block: 5″ × 5″

SKILL LEVEL: MODERATE

This quilt was inspired by many leftover pieces of backing strips that had been cut away from other quilts. What can be done with those long, often neutral, strips of fabric? This quilt is just one idea. Contrast creates the design. Notice that by grouping the lights together and the darks together, the overall pattern emerges. If both light and dark fabrics had been used in each block, the result would be much different.

MATERIALS

Dark scraps:
- 3⅝ yards total for blocks and border
- ⅝ yard total for appliqués

- **Light scraps:** 3¼ yards total for blocks and border
- **Green fabric:** ⅔ yard for bias vine
- **Brown fabric:** ¾ yard for inner borders

- **Backing:** 5 yards
- **Binding:** ⅔ yard
- **Batting:** 79″ × 89″
- **Freezer paper**

Strip Sets

When piecing blocks from strips, it's easier to sew strips together and then cut the blocks the size you need. Making several blocks from one strip set is faster than sewing blocks individually.

CUTTING

Strip widths and lengths are given below; however, you can improvise with what you have on hand. Even the tiniest strips can be used in this quilt. Use as many strips as needed until your strip sets are 5½″ wide or until you create blocks that are 5½″ × 5½″. All measurements include ¼″-wide seam allowances.

Make a template for the leaves, using the pattern (page 37) and referring to Making and Using Templates (page 96).

Dark scraps
- Cut 74 strips 1½″ × 18″.
- Cut 74 strips 2″ × 18″.

Light scraps
- Cut 64 strips 1½″ × 18″.
- Cut 64 strips 2″ × 18″.
- Cut 4 strips 2″ × 5½″.
- Cut 4 strips 1½″ × 5½″.

Dark scraps for appliqué
- Cut 124 leaves.

Green fabric
- Cut 1¼″-wide bias strips to total 272″.

Brown fabric
- Cut 12 strips 2″ × width of fabric.

Binding
- Cut 8 strips 2″ × width of fabric.

Block Assembly

Refer to Quiltmaking Basics (page 93) as needed.

1. Sew 2 dark 2″ × 18″ strips and 2 dark 1½″ × 18″ strips together lengthwise in any order. The finished strip set will be 5½″ wide. Press the seams in one direction. Make 37 strip sets, varying the order in which the strips are sewn together.

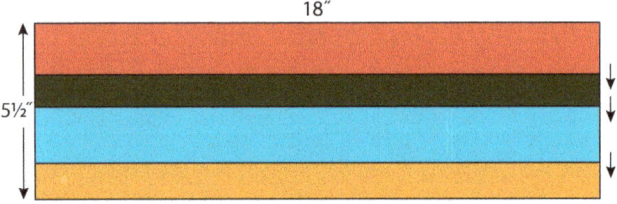

Make 37 strip sets.

2. Crosscut each strip set into 3 segments 5½″ wide to make the blocks. Cut 107 blocks total. The blocks should measure 5½″ × 5½″. Cut 4 segments 3″ × 5½″ for the half-blocks.

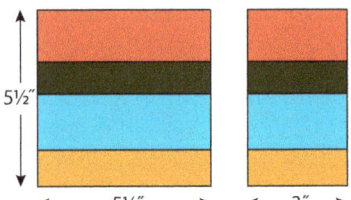

Cut 107 blocks and 4 half-blocks.

3. Repeat Steps 1 and 2 using the light 2″ × 18″ and 1½″ × 18″ strips. Cut 96 segments for the blocks; do not cut any half-blocks.

4. Sew a light 2″ × 5½″ strip to a light 1½″ × 5½″ strip to make a half-block. Press the seams to one side. Make 4 light half-blocks.

Make 4 half-blocks.

Border Assembly

Refer to the quilt assembly diagram (page 37) when assembling the borders.

Brown Border

1. Sew the 12 brown 2″ strips together end to end and press the seams open.

2. Cut 2 strips 55½″ for the inner left and right side borders.

3. Cut 2 strips 48½″ for the inner top and bottom borders.

4. Cut 2 strips 68½″ for the third left and right side borders.

5. Cut 2 strips 61½″ for the third top and bottom borders.

Pieced Borders

1. Sew 12 light blocks side by side to make the appliqué background border. Press the seams in one direction. Make 4.

2. Prepare the green bias strips, referring to Bias Stems (page 98). Set aside until you're ready to assemble the quilt.

3. Prepare the 124 leaves for appliqué, referring to Appliqué (page 96) as needed, and set aside.

4. Sew 15 dark blocks side by side to make the outer border. Press the seams in one direction. Make 4.

Quilt Assembly

1. Arrange and sew the blocks into 9 vertical rows as shown in the quilt assembly diagram (below). Note that the seams of the light blocks are horizontal and the seams of the dark blocks are vertical. Press the seams toward the light blocks.

2. Sew the rows together and press the seams in one direction.

3. Sew the brown 55½" borders to the left and right sides. Press the seams toward the borders. Sew the brown 48½" borders to the top and bottom. Press the seams toward the borders.

4. Trim the 4 pieced light borders to 58½" and sew to the sides of the quilt. Press the seams toward the brown border. Sew the remaining light borders to the top and bottom. Press the seams toward the brown border.

5. Sew the brown 2" × 68½" borders to the left and right sides of the quilt. Press the seams toward the brown strips. Sew the brown 2" × 61½" borders to the top and bottom. Press the seams toward the brown strips.

6. Arrange the bias strip in a curving line around the light borders, referring to the photograph (page 34) for placement guidance. Pin or baste in place and appliqué by machine or hand.

7. Arrange the leaves on the border. Pin or baste in position, and then use the method of your choice to machine or hand appliqué in place.

8. Trim the 4 pieced outer borders to 71½" and sew to the left and right sides of the quilt. Press the seams toward the brown border. Sew the outer borders to the top and bottom. Press the seams toward the brown border.

9. Stitch or baste along the outer edge of the border to stabilize the seams and prevent stretching during the quilting process.

10. Layer the quilt top, batting, and backing. Baste, quilt as desired, and bind. Refer to Quilt Finishing (page 98) for additional details.

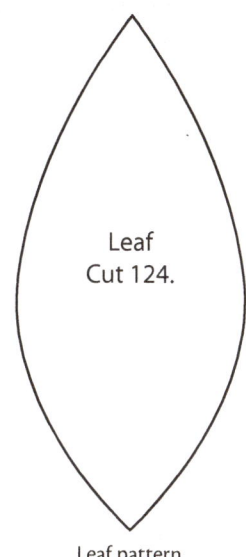

Leaf
Cut 124.

Leaf pattern

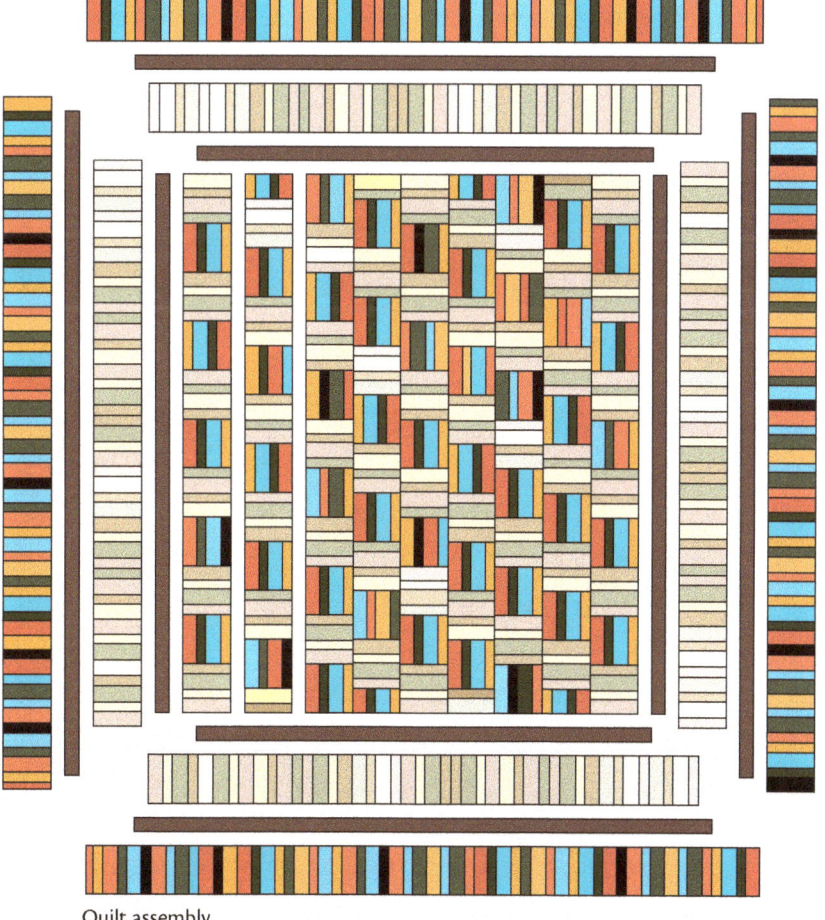

Quilt assembly

ZEPHYR

USING *Repetition*

So many quilters express frustration when looking at their scraps (or piles of fat quarters or bundles of precuts) because they simply see a jumble of colors and prints. Almost any fabric can be combined with another in the same quilt when you use the design secret of repetition. Repetition of blocks, colors, or shapes can provide consistency without limiting the variety of scraps you use.

Maybe one of the quilts in this book will be the answer for your scraps. Read through the following discussions of repeating elements in quilts and you will see them in a whole new way. Then look at your stash again—who knows what those fabrics will inspire!

Block Pattern

Almost any block, or even two blocks, can create a larger pattern when they are lined up in rows. The way the blocks interact with the ones next to them allows an overall design to be created. Whether the blocks are simple squares, triangles, or something more complex, they create patterns where they meet. These are often called secondary patterns. The repetition of the blocks or alternate blocks pulls the scrappy fabrics together in a way that makes them look like they belong with each other. *Fusion* (page 40) uses only three colors, but imagine this quilt in a wide array of colors. The pattern would still be the same, because it's created by the intersections of the blocks and the alternate blocks and repeated throughout the quilt.

Scraps and precut fabric bundle

Secondary patterns created by 2 blocks in *Fusion*

Color

If you strategically place a bit of one fabric (or color) in each block, you'll be surprised at the effect it can have. One color or several shades of one color can create a calming and mellow effect. By repeating the same colors in the same places in each block, a rhythm emerges. Repetition of color gives consistency to a design that would otherwise be less obvious. Repeated colors can create an overall pattern that would not appear if random colors were used.

Repetition of color in *Paper Chain* (page 48) gives consistency.

Shape

Dig through your scraps and what do you see? If there's too much variety of color or pattern, you need another option to make them work together. Choosing a shape to repeat in the blocks, sashing, cornerstones, and/or borders will make something fun happen. All these fabrics can work together by repeating a common shape. *Sawnee Shadows* (page 44) uses triangles in two sizes, but how about rectangles? Or hexagons? The simple repetition of the basic shapes creates the calm that a variety of scraps often needs. Many different fabrics made into many different blocks would be a bit too chaotic.

Triangle shapes in *Sawnee Shadows* provide order to multiple prints and colors.

FUSION

Pieced by Diane D. Knott and machine quilted by Betty Alonsious

Finished quilt: 60″ × 70″

Finished block: 5″ × 5″

SKILL LEVEL: EASY

Not only are the two blocks in this quilt repeated in alternating rows, but the secondary design that they create also repeats. When you look at *Fusion*, do you see the individual blocks, or the pattern created by the blocks merging together? I'm currently saving my scraps to make this quilt again, using homespuns and plaids. It would also be perfect to make in school colors for a dorm room!

MATERIALS

- **Red scraps:** 1¾ yards total
- **Gray scraps:** 2¼ yards total
- **White scraps:** 2 yards total
- **Backing:** 4 yards
- **Binding:** ⅝ yard
- **Batting:** 68″ × 78″

CUTTING

All measurements include ¼″-wide seam allowances.

Red scraps
- Cut 26 rectangles 3″ × 5½″ for border blocks.
- Cut 72 matching pairs of squares 3½″ × 3½″ for Square-in-a-Square blocks.

Gray scraps
- Cut 72 squares 3″ × 3″ for Square-in-a-Square blocks.
- Cut 36 squares 6¼″ × 6¼″ for Hourglass blocks.
- Cut 22 rectangles 3″ × 5½″ for border blocks.
- Cut 4 squares 3″ × 3″ for border corners.

White scraps
- Cut 36 squares 6¼″ × 6¼″ for Hourglass blocks.
- Cut 72 matching pairs of squares 2⅝″ × 2⅝″ for Square-in-a-Square blocks.

Binding
- Cut 7 strips 2″ × width of fabric.

tip

Keep It Simple

Do you want to make a particular quilt but it looks too difficult? Simplify it by taking a complex block and reducing the number of pieces or seams, or even enlarging it. This will make it much easier to tackle and will also give the quilt a modern, updated feel.

Square-in-a-Square Block Assembly

Refer to Quiltmaking Basics (page 93) as needed. For each block, choose 1 gray 3″ × 3″ square, 2 matching white 2⅝″ × 2⅝″ squares, and 2 matching red 3½″ × 3½″ squares.

1. Cut the 2 white squares and 2 red squares in half on the diagonal, creating 4 triangles of each.

2. Sew a white triangle to opposite sides of the 3″ × 3″ gray square. Press the seams toward the square.

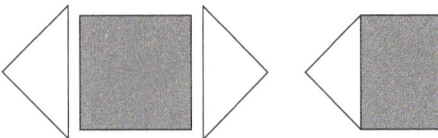

3. Repeat to sew 2 white triangles to the remaining sides of the square. Press the seams toward the white fabric.

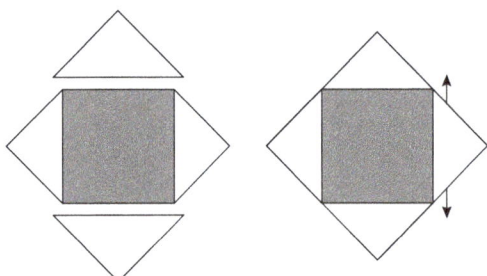

4. Sew a red triangle to opposite sides of the unit from Step 3. Press the seams toward the red fabric.

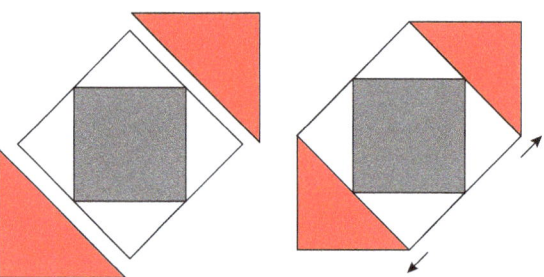

5. Repeat to sew 2 red triangles to the remaining sides of the block. The block should measure 5½″ × 5½″. Repeat Steps 1–5 to make a total of 72 blocks.

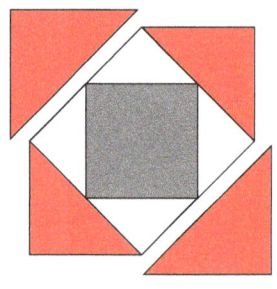 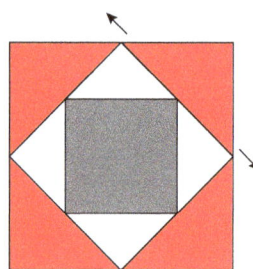

Make 72.

Hourglass Block Assembly

1. Layer 1 gray 6¼″ square and 1 white 6¼″ square right sides together. Mark the diagonal and make 2 half-square triangle units (page 95). Press the seams toward the gray fabric.

2. Layer the 2 half-square triangle units, right sides together, with the gray facing the white and white facing the gray. Snug the seams together and pin along the seam. On the wrong side of one of the units, draw a diagonal line from corner to corner using a pencil; the line should be perpendicular to the seam. Sew ¼″ from the drawn line on both sides. Cut on the drawn line to make 2 Hourglass blocks.

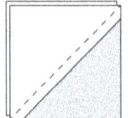 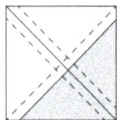 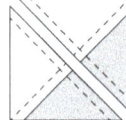

Layer, mark, sew, and cut.

3. Pinwheel-press the seams (page 94). The block should measure 5½″ × 5½″. Repeat Steps 1–3 to make 71 blocks.

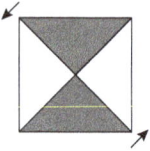 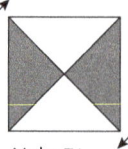

Make 71.

Quilt Assembly

1. Arrange the blocks in 13 rows of 11 blocks each, alternating the blocks as shown in the quilt assembly diagram.

2. Add the red and gray 3″ × 5½″ rectangles to the ends of the rows and along the top and bottom. Add a gray 3″ square to each corner.

3. Sew the blocks into rows, including the border rectangles. Press the seams toward the Hourglass blocks.

4. Sew the top and bottom borders into rows with the gray 3″ × 3″ squares on each end. Press the seams toward the red fabrics.

5. Sew the rows together.

6. Layer the quilt top, batting, and backing. Baste, quilt as desired, and bind. Refer to Quilt Finishing (page 98) for additional details.

Quilt assembly

FUSION 43

SAWNEE SHADOWS

Pieced and machine quilted by Diane D. Knott

Finished quilt: 55″ × 72″
Finished block: 5″ × 12″

SKILL LEVEL: MODERATE

A great set of hiking trails that climb Sawnee Mountain is very close to my home. I am often intrigued by the way the sun reflects through the trees and casts shadows at different times of day. This quilt was inspired by some of those shadows I saw while hiking. Imagine using black backgrounds and batik scraps, or a white background with scraps in shades of red and pink. They would create vibrant alternatives to this pattern.

MATERIALS

- **Dark scraps:** 4 yards total
- **Light scraps:** 2½ yards total
- **Backing:** 3½ yards
- **Binding:** ¾ yard
- **Batting:** 63″ × 80″
- **Freezer paper**

CUTTING

Make templates, using patterns A and B (page 47) and referring to Making and Using Templates (page 96). All measurements include ¼"-wide seam allowances.

Dark scraps
- Cut 126 of template A.*
- Cut 126 of template B.**

Light scraps
- Cut 378 of template A* (126 sets of 3 matching pieces).

Binding
- Cut bias strips 2″ wide to total 300″.

* If your scraps are large enough, these can be cut from 3½" strips.
** If your scraps are large enough, these can be cut from 6½" strips.

>  **Tidy Tip**
>
> *Organize pieces in stacks to save time and frustration. Move stacks from the cutting table to the sewing area by placing them on a wide ruler or a small cutting mat for easy transportation.*

Block Assembly

Refer to Quiltmaking Basics (page 93) as needed.

1. Arrange 3 matching small light triangles and 1 small dark triangle as shown. Sew the light triangles to the small dark triangle and press the seams toward the light background to make a half-block.

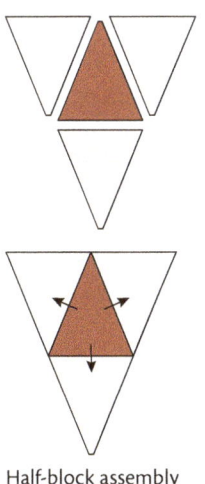

Half-block assembly

2. Sew the half-block to a large triangle to complete the block. Press the seams toward the large triangle. Repeat Steps 1 and 2 to make a total of 116 blocks.

3. Repeat Step 1 to make 10 half-blocks.

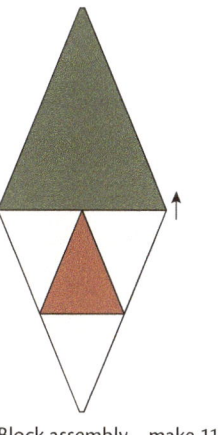

Block assembly—make 116.

SAWNEE SHADOWS 45

Quilt Assembly

1. Arrange the blocks, half-blocks, and remaining 10 dark triangles into diagonal rows, referring to the quilt assembly diagram (at right).

2. Sew the blocks together into diagonal rows, aligning the raw edges and ends so that the ¼" seam intersections align. Press the seams in opposite directions from row to row.

3. Sew the rows together. Press the seams open.

4. Layer the quilt top, batting, and backing. Baste, quilt as desired, and bind. Refer to Quilt Finishing (page 98) for additional details.

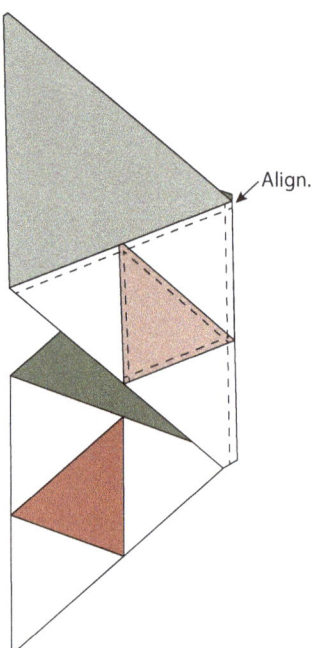

Sew blocks together.

Quilt assembly

Zigzag Binding

The binding for this quilt follows the shape of the blocks and will be easier to apply if you cut the strips on the bias. It is applied in a manner similar to regular binding. Treat the points the same as the corners of any quilt by simply folding the binding back, then folding it back down and aligning it with the next edge of the quilt. Snip the seam allowance at the inside corners to help the binding lie flat after it's turned to the back of the quilt. Take care not to snip into the stitching.

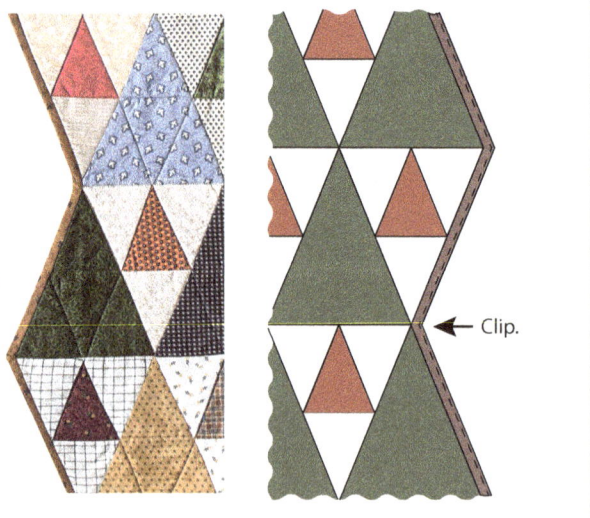

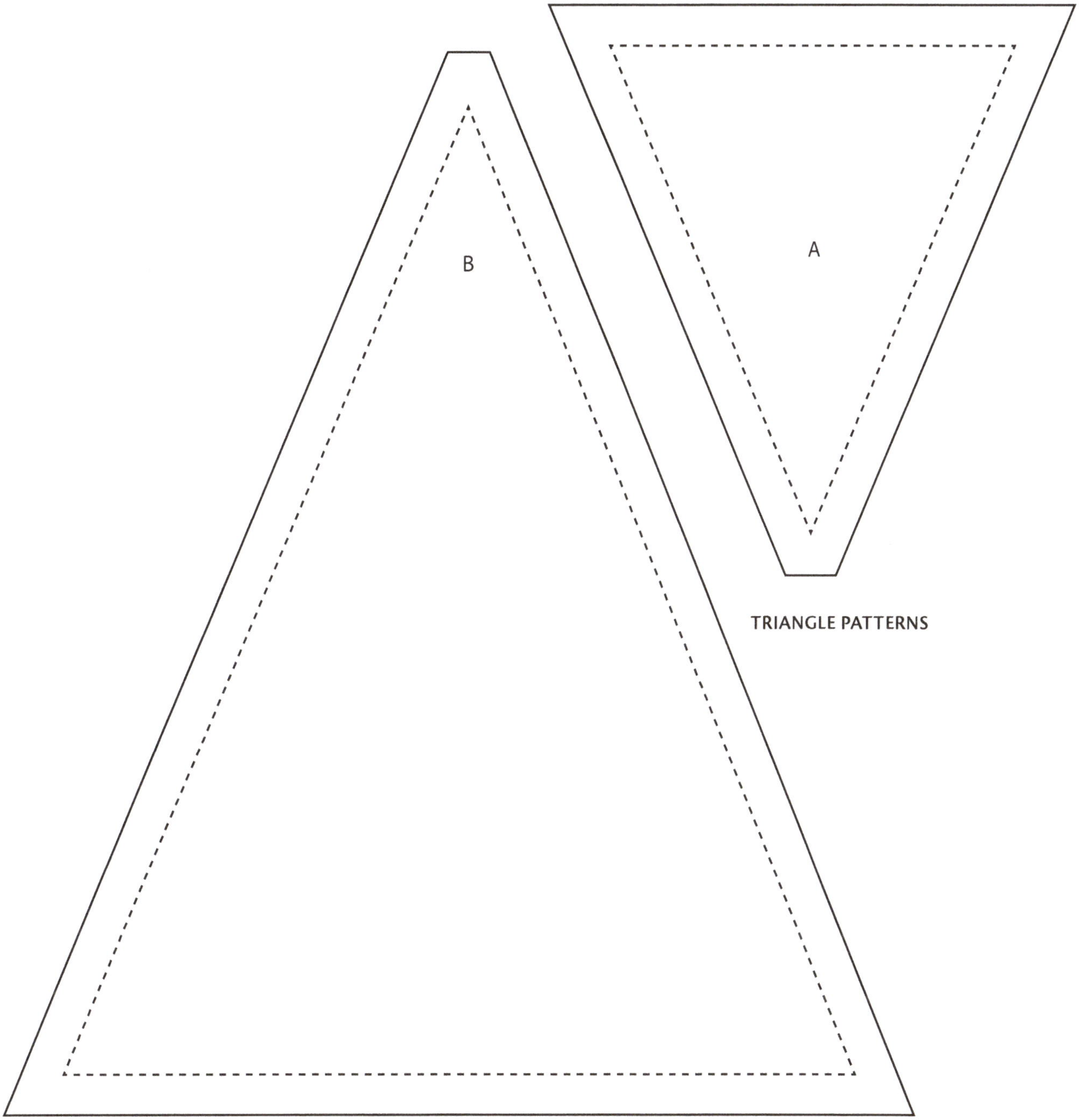

B

A

TRIANGLE PATTERNS

SAWNEE SHADOWS 47

PAPER CHAIN

Pieced by Diane D. Knott and machine quilted by Betty Alonsious

Finished quilt: 70¼″ × 87¼″

Finished block: 4″ × 4″

SKILL LEVEL: MODERATE

Making paper chains from colorful construction paper strips was one of my favorite activities as a child. I wanted to make a quilt that reminded me of those paper chains. I began designing with simple Four-Patch and Drunkard's Path blocks set on point. Note that the Four-Patch blocks all have the lightest fabric (yellow) on top, the medium fabrics (orange) on both sides, and the darker fabric (red) on the bottom. By repeating the color placements, a woven effect emerges. High contrast between the chain pieces and the background really shows off the pattern.

MATERIALS

- **Cream scraps:** 3¼ yards total for backgrounds
- **Yellow scraps:** ½ yard total for Four-Patch blocks
- **Orange scraps:** ⅞ yard total for Four-Patch blocks
- **Red scraps:** 1¾ yards total for blocks
- **Border fabric:** 2⅜ yards
- **Backing:** 5⅓ yards
- **Binding:** ¾ yard
- **Batting:** 79″ × 96″
- **Freezer paper**

CUTTING

Make templates for A and B, using the patterns (page 51) and referring to Making and Using Templates (page 96). All measurements include ¼″-wide seam allowances.

Cream scraps
- Cut 70 squares 4½″ × 4½″.
- Cut 130 squares 4½″ × 4½″; from the squares cut 130 of template A.

Yellow scraps
- Cut 84 squares 2½″ × 2½″.

Orange scraps
- Cut 168 squares 2½″ × 2½″.

Red scraps
- Cut 84 squares 2½″ × 2½″.
- Cut 130 squares 3½″ × 3½″; from the squares cut 130 of template B.

Border
- Cut 2 strips* 4½″ × 79¾″.
- Cut 2 strips* 4½″ × 70¾″.
- Cut 2 squares 4¼″ × 4¼″; cut in half diagonally to make 4 corner triangles.
- Cut 12 squares 8″ × 8″; cut in quarters diagonally to make 48 setting triangles (2 are extra).

Binding
- Cut 9 strips 2″ × width of fabric.

*You may want to cut the border strips a couple inches longer, measure the quilt center after it is complete, and then cut the strips to fit.

Four-Patch Assembly

Refer to Quiltmaking Basics (page 93) as needed.

1. Arrange 1 yellow 2½″ square, 2 orange 2½″ squares, and 1 red 2½″ square as shown. Sew 2 rows of 2 squares. Press the seams toward the orange fabric.

2. Sew the rows together. Pinwheel-press the seams (page 94).

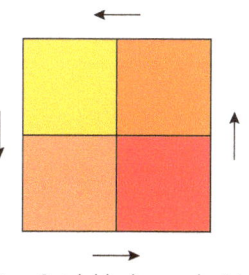

Four-Patch blocks—make 84.

Drunkard's Path Block Assembly

Refer to Sewing Curves (below).

1. Match the centers of piece A and piece B and pin, right sides together.

2. Sew a ¼" seam along the curve, with the background piece on top. Press the seams toward the red fabric.

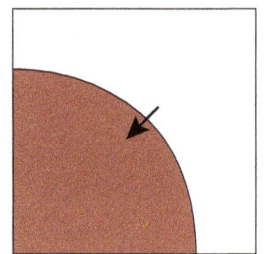

Drunkard's Path block—make 130.

 **SEWING CURVES**

Sewing curves is easy as long as you take your time and sew carefully!

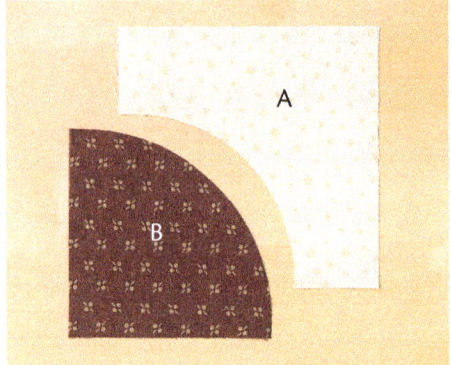

A and B pieces for Drunkard's Path block

1. *Fold the A and B pieces in half to find the centers of the curves and finger-press a crease. Fold one piece with right sides together and the other piece with wrong sides together.*

2. *Pin the center first, then the ends, and then add pins between each.*

3. *Sew slowly with the background piece on top. Let the machine feed the fabric, using very gentle pressure to guide it. When making adjustments, stop with the needle in the down position. Be sure to take your time. It's faster than resewing mistakes!*

Quilt Assembly

1. Arrange the blocks and cream 4½" squares in diagonal rows as shown in the quilt assembly diagram (at right). Add the side and corner setting triangles. *Note: Place the yellow of each Four-Patch block at the **top** to create the pattern.*

2. Sew the blocks into rows, including the setting triangles. Press the seams in opposite direction from row to row.

3. Sew the rows together. Trim the edges as needed, being careful to leave at least a ¼" seam allowance beyond the points of the Four-Patch blocks. The quilt center should measure 62¾" × 79¾".

4. Sew the 4½" × 79¾" borders to the left and right sides of the quilt. Press the seams toward the borders.

5. Sew the 4½" × 70¾" borders to the top and bottom of the quilt. Press the seams toward the borders.

6. Layer the quilt top, batting, and backing. Baste, quilt as desired, and bind. Refer to Quilt Finishing (page 98) for additional details.

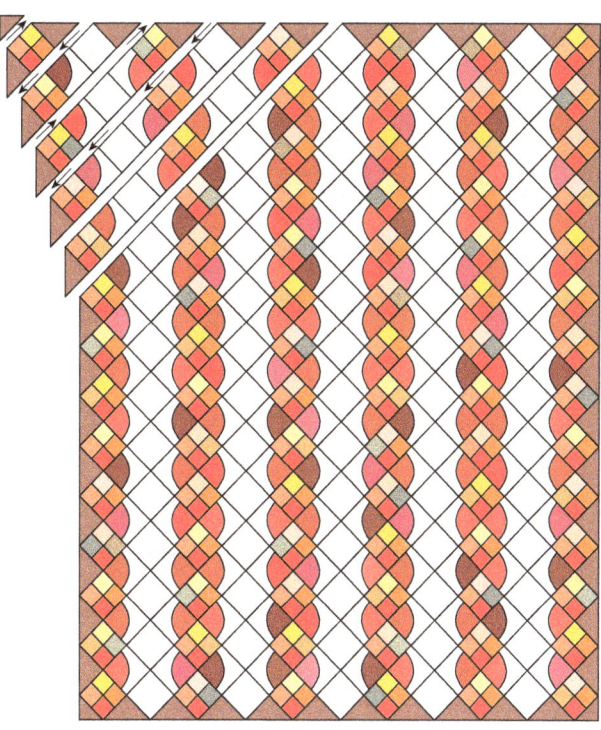

Quilt assembly

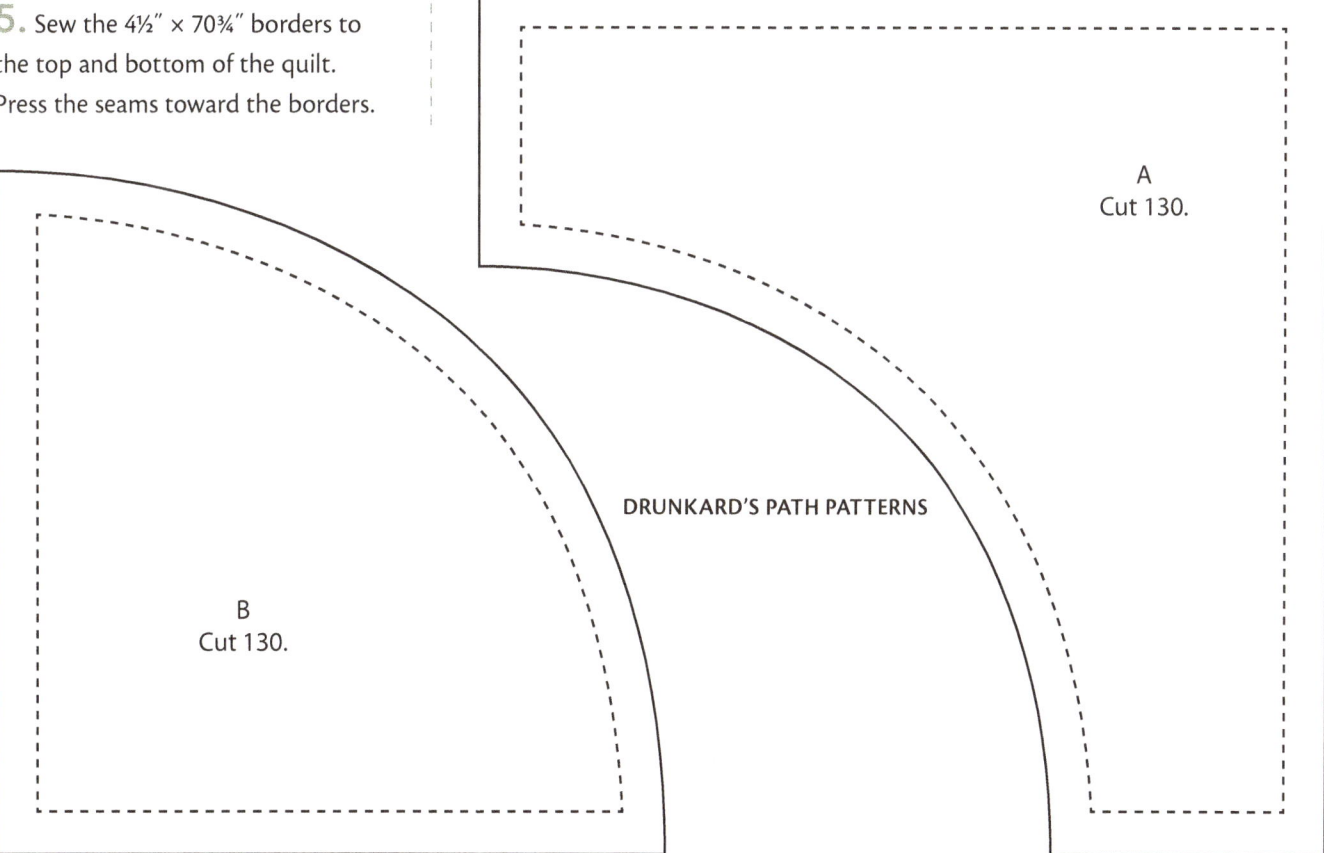

DRUNKARD'S PATH PATTERNS

A Cut 130.

B Cut 130.

PAPER CHAIN 51

USING *Accents*

Choosing an accent color and using it well can make a huge difference in a quilt design. Having twin boys, I often make the same quilt for both of them. However, I use blue as an accent for one and red for the other. The quilts look totally different but coexist nicely on twin beds in the same room. Using an accent color in a scrap quilt is the most satisfying way to get random scraps to play together nicely. The small amount of "pop" really can make a quilt sparkle.

Selecting an accent color is so important that it's the perfect excuse to give yourself permission to go fabric shopping. I know you're trying to use up your scraps, but every once in a while, your scraps need that one special purchase of a new fabric to bring them all together. If you buy a yard of fabric and it allows you to use up several yards of scraps, aren't you still coming out ahead? Exactly! Besides, who doesn't love a trip to the nearest quilt shop?

Fabric scraps with accent fabric

FOUR-PATCH PLAID

Pieced by Diane D. Knott and machine quilted by Betty Alonsious

Finished quilt: 66˝ × 76½˝

Finished block: 9˝ × 9˝

SKILL LEVEL: EASY

This quilt was made almost entirely of Four-Patch blocks. I used up every 2˝ square and 2˝ strip I had in my stash at the time. The finished blocks needed something to separate them, so I chose the dark orange fabric as an accent fabric for the sashing. This quilt would have looked completely different but just as wonderful if I used dark blue or green sashing. This pattern is perfect for featuring holiday colors.

FOUR-PATCH PLAID 53

MATERIALS

- **Light scraps:** 1½ yards total
- **Dark scraps:** 4 yards total
- **Blue scraps:** ¼ yard total
- **Orange fabric:** 1⅛ yards
- **Backing:** 4¾ yards
- **Binding:** ⅔ yard
- **Batting:** 74″ × 85″

Accentuate the Accent

After you've decided on your accent color for the sashing, consider the color on the opposite side of the color wheel for the sashing cornerstones. In my quilt, I chose scraps in blue, which is opposite of orange on the color wheel.

CUTTING

All measurements include ¼″-wide seam allowances.

Light scraps
- Cut 480 squares 2″ × 2″.

Dark scraps
- Cut 600 squares 2″ × 2″.
- Cut 116 strips 2″ × 13″.

Blue scraps
- Cut 42 squares 2″ × 2″.

Orange fabric
- Cut 4 strips 9½″ × width of fabric; subcut 71 strips 2″ × 9½″.

Binding
- Cut 8 strips 2″ × width of fabric.

Four-Patch Assembly

Refer to Quiltmaking Basics (page 93) as needed.

1. Sew 4 light 2″ × 2″ squares together in pairs. Press the seams in opposite directions.

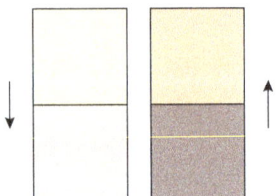

2. Sew the 2 units together to make a four-patch. Pinwheel-press the seams (page 94). The unit should measure 3½″ × 3½″. Repeat to make 120 units with 4 light squares and 150 units with 4 dark squares.

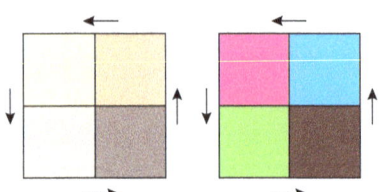

Four-patch unit—make 120 light and 150 dark.

Nine-Patch Block Assembly

Each block requires 5 dark four-patch units and 4 light four-patch units.

1. Arrange the four-patch units into a Nine-Patch block, as shown. Sew the units into 3 rows of 3 four-patch units. Press the seams as shown.

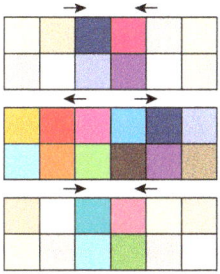

2. Sew the rows together. Press the seams as shown. The block should measure 9½" × 9½".

Nine-Patch block—make 30.

Border Assembly

1. Sew 4 dark 2" × 13" strips together to make a strip set. Press the seams in one direction. Make 29 strip sets. Cut each strip set into 6 segments 2" wide for a total of 174 segments.

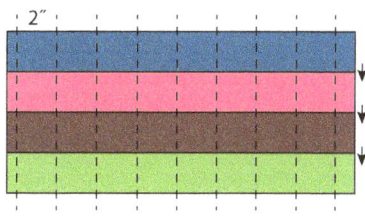

Make 29 strip sets. Cut 174 segments.

2. Sew the segments together to make the borders, rotating them so that the seam allowances will nest together. Make 2 borders with 43 segments each and 2 borders with 44 segments each. Press the seams in one direction.

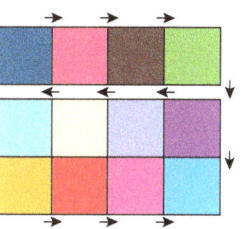

Quilt Assembly

1. Arrange the blocks, sashing strips, and cornerstones as shown in the quilt assembly diagram (below).

2. Sew the blocks and sashing strips into rows. Press the seams toward the sashing strips. Sew the sashing and cornerstones into rows; press toward the sashing.

3. Sew the rows together and press the seams toward the sashing rows.

4. Sew the borders with 43 segments to the sides of the quilt. Press the seams toward the sashing.

5. Sew the borders with 44 segments to the top and bottom. Press the seams toward the sashing.

6. Layer the quilt top, batting, and backing. Baste, quilt as desired, and bind. Refer to Quilt Finishing (page 98) for additional details.

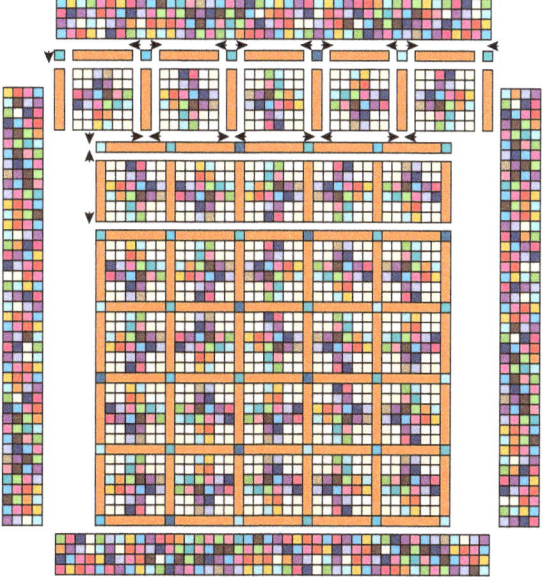

Quilt assembly

FOUR-PATCH PLAID

DETOUR

Pieced and machine quilted by Diane D. Knott

Finished quilt: 72″ × 96″

Finished block: 12″ × 12″

SKILL LEVEL: EASY

Let's be honest—sometimes you just have to buy what's left on a bolt of fabric. It doesn't matter why; it just happens. I bought this blue fabric because of the unusual shade of blue and the tiny check pattern. It happened to be on sale, too. Using this accent fabric allowed my huge variety of scraps to play nicely together. Without an accent, this quilt could look messy and confusing. Go find one of those special pieces of fabric, either in your stash or at the quilt shop, and build a scrap quilt around it!

MATERIALS

- **Light scraps:** 3½ yards total
- **Dark scraps:** 3¼ yards total
- **Blue check fabric:** 2 yards
- **Backing:** 6 yards
- **Batting:** 80˝ × 104˝

tip
Color Search

Having a hard time deciding on an accent color? Choose your favorite fabric, or go buy a piece of fabric that you've been wanting, and add scraps that coordinate with or complement it. You'll end up with a combination that you love!

CUTTING

All measurements include ¼˝-wide seam allowances.

Light scraps
- Cut 96 squares 2˝ × 2˝.
- Cut 48 strips 2˝ × 3½˝.
- Cut 48 strips 2˝ × 5˝.
- Cut 48 strips 2˝ × 6½˝.
- Cut 48 strips 2˝ × 8˝.
- Cut 48 strips 2˝ × 9½˝.
- Cut 48 strips 2˝ × 11˝.

Dark scraps
- Cut 48 strips 2˝ × 3½˝.
- Cut 48 strips 2˝ × 5˝.
- Cut 48 strips 2˝ × 6½˝.
- Cut 48 strips 2˝ × 8˝.
- Cut 48 strips 2˝ × 9½˝.
- Cut 48 strips 2˝ × 11˝.

Blue check
- Cut 20 strips 2˝ × width of fabric; subcut 384 squares 2˝ × 2˝.
- Cut 9 strips 2˝ × width of fabric for the binding.

Block Assembly

Refer to Quiltmaking Basics (page 93) as needed. Each block requires 8 blue squares, 2 light squares, a light strip of each size, and a dark strip of each size.

1. Sew 2 blue squares and 2 light squares together in pairs and press toward the blue. Sew the units into a four-patch unit. Pinwheel-press the seams (page 94).

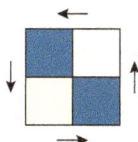

2. Sew a light 2˝ × 3½˝ strip to one side of the four-patch. Sew a dark 2˝ × 3½˝ strip to the opposite side. Press the seams toward the strips.

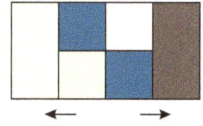

3. Sew a blue square to the end of a light 2˝ × 5˝ strip and a dark 2˝ × 5˝ strip. Press the seams away from the blue square.

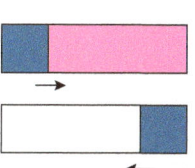

4. Sew the Step 3 units to opposite sides of the Step 2 unit as shown so that a diagonal chain of blue squares begins to form. Press the seams toward the strips just added.

5. Sew a light 2″ × 6½″ strip to the light side of the unit from Step 4. Sew a dark 2″ × 6½″ strip to the dark side of the unit. Press the seams toward the strips just added.

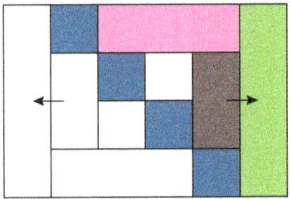

6. Sew a blue square to the end of a light 2″ × 8″ strip and a dark 2″ × 8″ strip. Press the seams away from the blue square.

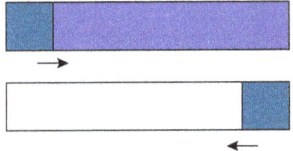

7. Sew the Step 6 units to the Step 5 unit, keeping light next to light and dark next to dark. Press the seams toward the units just added.

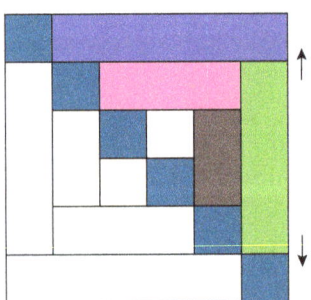

8. Sew a light 2″ × 9½″ strip to the light side of the block, and sew a dark 2″ × 9½″ strip to the dark side of the block. Press the seams toward the strips just added.

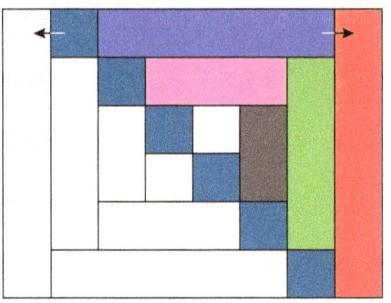

9. Sew a blue square to the end of a light 2″ × 11″ strip and a dark 2″ × 11″ strip. Press the seams away from the blue square.

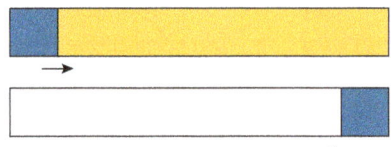

10. Sew the light unit from Step 9 to the light side of the block and the dark unit to the dark side of the block. Press the seams toward the strip just added. The block should measure 12½″ × 12½″. Repeat the steps to make 48 blocks.

Make 48.

Quilt Assembly

1. Arrange the blocks in 8 rows of 6 blocks each, referring to the quilt assembly diagram.

2. Sew the blocks into rows. Press the seams in each row in alternating directions.

3. Sew the rows together and press the seams open.

4. Layer the quilt top, batting, and backing. Baste, quilt as desired, and bind. Refer to Quilt Finishing (page 98) for additional details.

Change It Up

For queen size, make 16 additional blocks and add a block to the left and right sides of each row.

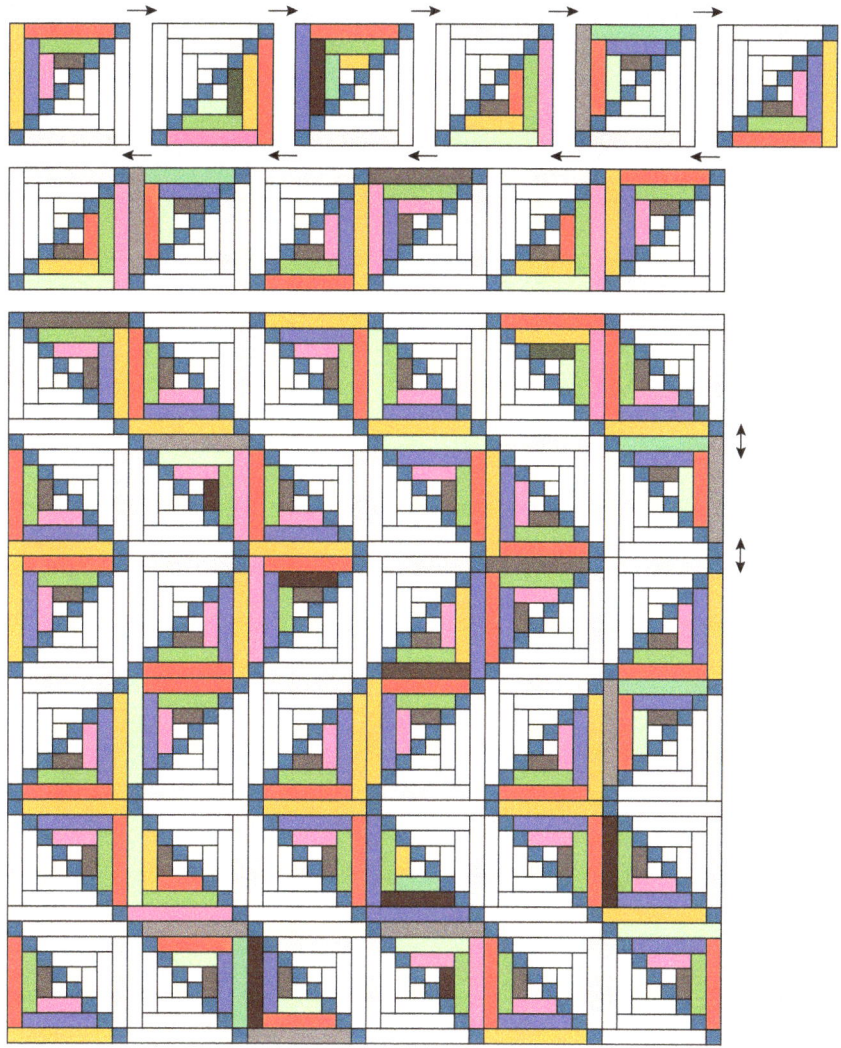

Quilt assembly

DETOUR 59

RAZZMATAZZ

Pieced by Diane D. Knott and quilted by Betty Alonsious

Finished quilt: 84″ × 84″

Finished block: 10½″ × 10½″

SKILL LEVEL: CHALLENGING

I've been making baby quilts using 1930s reproduction prints for years. While I had a huge variety of scraps left over, none of the pieces were very large. What was I going to do with so many tiny pieces that were too cute to throw out? This pattern is perfect for those cherished bits of fabric that are not big enough for most blocks. This traditional pattern could be made without scraps, but the variety of colors and prints adds a real sparkle to the design, don't you agree?

MATERIALS

- **Light print scraps:** 3½ yards total
- **Dark raspberry solid:** 6 yards
- **Orange print:** 2⅛ yards
- **White fabric:** 1⅞ yards
- **Backing:** 7¾ yards
- **Batting:** 92″ × 92″
- **Paper for foundation piecing**
- **Freezer paper**
- **Add-A-Quarter ruler** (*optional*)

 Pattern Alternative
If you prefer, you can make the pieced arcs in this block by cutting the scraps individually with a template and then sewing by hand or machine. However, paper piecing allows you to skip the template cutting and makes the arc perfect every time.

CUTTING

Make templates for pieces A and B, using the patterns (pages 65 and 66) and referring to Making and Using Templates (page 96). All measurements include ¼″-wide seam allowances.

Light scraps
- Cut 880 rectangles 1¾″ × 3″.*

Dark raspberry
- Cut 736 rectangles 1¾″ × 3″.*
- Cut 3 strips 11″ × width of fabric; subcut 40 strips 2½″ × 11″.
- Cut 10 strips 2½″ × width of fabric for Nine-Patch blocks.
- Cut 9 strips 2½″ × width of fabric for borders.
- Cut 9 strips 2″ × width of fabric for binding.

Orange print
- Cut 64 of template B.
- Cut 8 strips 2½″ × width of fabric for Nine-Patch blocks.
- Cut 8 strips 2½″ × width of fabric for borders.

White
- Cut 16 of template A.
- Cut 8 strips 2½″ × width of fabric for borders.

* *These pieces are for paper foundation piecing and do not need to be extremely precise. You may find that 1½″ × 3″ pieces are big enough after you get the hang of the technique.*

RAZZMATAZZ

Paper Piecing the Arcs

You'll use a simple sew-and-flip method of foundation piecing. The patterns are marked with an R to indicate where the dark raspberry fabric should be placed.

1. Make 64 copies of the fan pattern C (page 66) onto paper for foundation piecing and cut them out along the outer lines.

2. Place a light 1¾" × 3" scrap on the end of the arc, right side up on the unmarked side. Pin in place over space 1. Hold the piece up to the light to make sure you have adequate seam allowance on all sides of the space. Place a dark raspberry 1¾" × 3" rectangle right sides together with the light rectangle; hold it up to the light again and adjust it so that it is approximately ¼" beyond the line between spaces 1 and 2. Pin in place. Turn the paper so that the printed side is facing up and sew on the printed line between spaces 1 and 2.

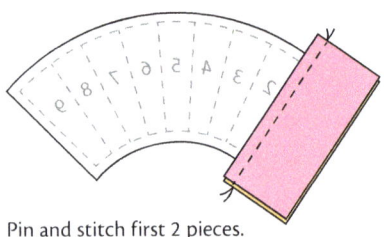

Pin and stitch first 2 pieces.

3. Turn the paper over and flip open the fabrics. Finger-press the seam or use a wooden pressing tool.

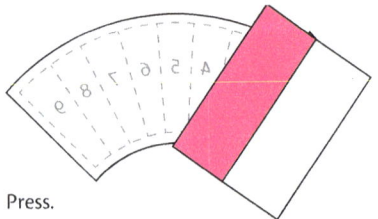

Press.

4. Fold the paper back along the next dotted line. Place it on a cutting mat and use a ruler and rotary cutter to trim away the excess fabric from the dark raspberry fabric, leaving a ¼" seam allowance.

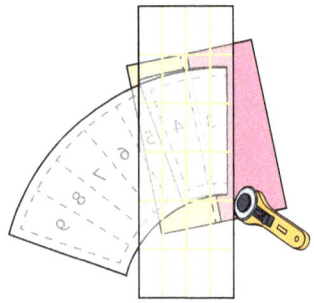

Cut ¼" past fold.

5. Unfold the paper and place a light scrap right sides together with the raspberry fabric, aligning the raw edge of the light scrap with the newly trimmed edge of the raspberry piece. Pin in place

6. Flip the paper to the printed side and sew along the dotted line. Repeat Steps 2–4 until the foundation is covered with alternating light scrap and dark raspberry fan blades.

7. After all the pieces are sewn to the foundation, trim the fabric even with the solid outer line. Do not remove the paper backing yet. Repeat Steps 2–6 to make 64 arcs.

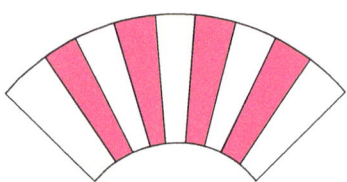

Completed arc—make 64.

Secrets to Perfect Paper Piecing

* Always make copies from the original pattern to prevent distortion.

* Measure the copies to ensure they are the correct size.

* For easier tearing, use paper designed for paper piecing, such as Carol Doak's Foundation Paper (see Resources, page 111), or use the lightest-weight copy paper you have available.

* Shorten the stitch length to 1.8–2.0, depending on your machine.

* Finger-press each seam before trimming the next piece. A wooden seam-pressing tool, sometimes called a "little wooden iron," is very useful for this.

* Trim the entire unit to size before removing the paper.

* Gently remove the paper by pinching the beginning of the seam while tearing away the paper.

Grandmother's Fan Block Assembly

Refer to Sewing Curves (page 50) as needed.

1. Gently remove the paper from the pieced arcs. Sew an orange print B piece to a paper-pieced arc (C). Press the seams toward B. Make 4.

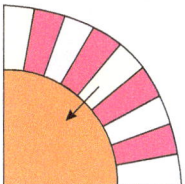
Make 4.

> **tip**
>
> **Stitch Setting**
>
> *When changing stitch settings on your machine, always take a photo of the settings. If you need to turn off your machine or finish stitching later, you will have an instant reference to the settings that were used.*

2. Fold piece A and the B/C units in half to find the center and finger press a crease. Matching the centers, pin and sew B/C units to opposite sides of a white piece A. Sew with the A piece on top and ease the fabric as you go to avoid tucks. Press the seams toward the B/C units.

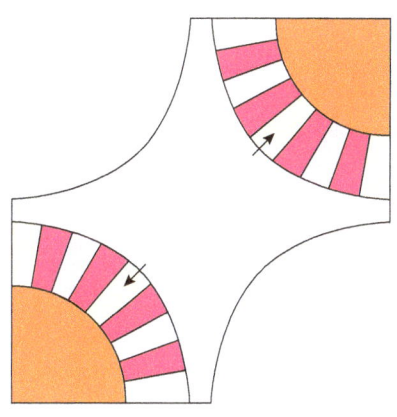

3. Repeat to sew 2 B/C units to the remaining sides of piece A and press the seams toward the B/C units. The block should measure 11″ × 11″. Repeat the steps to make a total of 16 blocks.

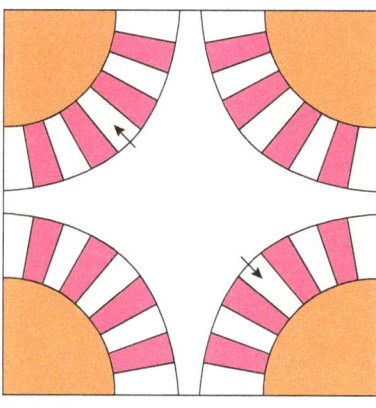
Make 16.

Sashing Assembly

1. Make 80 copies of the sashing pattern D (page 67) onto paper for foundation piecing and cut them out along the outer lines.

2. Beginning with a light 1¾″ × 3″ scrap on the end of the foundation marked 1, follow the steps Paper Piecing the Arcs (page 62) to piece the sashing rectangle. Trim the edges even with the outer line of the foundation paper after all of the pieces are sewn. Make 80 pieced sashing units.

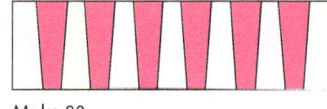
Make 80.

3. Sew a pieced sashing unit to each side of a 2½″ × 11″ dark raspberry sashing strip. Be sure that the wider ends of the light prints are next to the center strip, as shown. Press the seams toward the raspberry strip. Make 40.

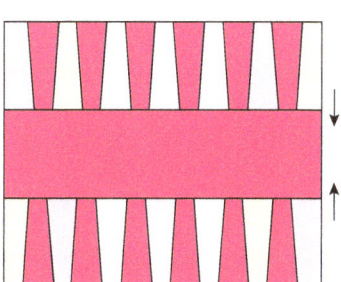
Sashing—make 40.

4. Carefully remove the paper from the back of the paper-pieced units. The units should measure 6½″ × 11″.

RAZZMATAZZ

Nine-Patch Block

Refer to Quiltmaking Basics (page 93) as needed.

1. Sew an orange 2½˝ × 42˝ strip between 2 dark raspberry 2½˝ strips to make a strip set. Press the seams toward the raspberry strips. Make 4 strip sets and cut 50 segments 2½˝ wide.

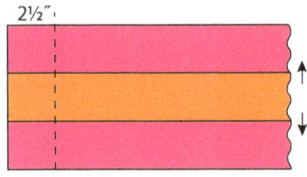

Make 4 strip sets; cut 50 segments.

2. Sew a dark raspberry 2½˝ × 42˝ strip between 2 orange 2½˝ strips to make a strip set. Press the seams toward the raspberry strip. Make 2 strip sets and cut 25 segments 2½˝ wide.

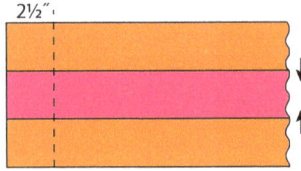

Make 2 strip sets; cut 25 segments.

3. Arrange 2 segments from Step 1 and 1 segment from Step 2 as shown. Sew the segments together and press the seams away from the center row. Make a total of 25 blocks. The blocks should measure 6½˝ × 6½˝.

Nine-Patch assembly—make 25.

Border Assembly

1. Sew the white border strips end to end and cut 2 borders 72½˝ long and 2 borders 76½˝ long.

2. Sew the orange border strips end to end and cut 2 borders 76½˝ long and 2 borders 80½˝ long.

3. Sew the dark raspberry border strips end to end and cut 2 borders 80½˝ long and 2 borders 84½˝ long.

Quilt Assembly

1. Arrange the Grandmother's Fan blocks, sashing units, and Nine-Patch blocks according to the quilt assembly diagram (below). Sew the units together into rows and press away from the sashing.

2. Sew the rows together. Press away from the sashing rows.

3. Add the white border and press the seams toward the border. Repeat with the orange and then the dark raspberry borders.

4. Layer the quilt top, batting, and backing. Baste, quilt as desired, and bind. Refer to Quilt Finishing (page 98) for additional details.

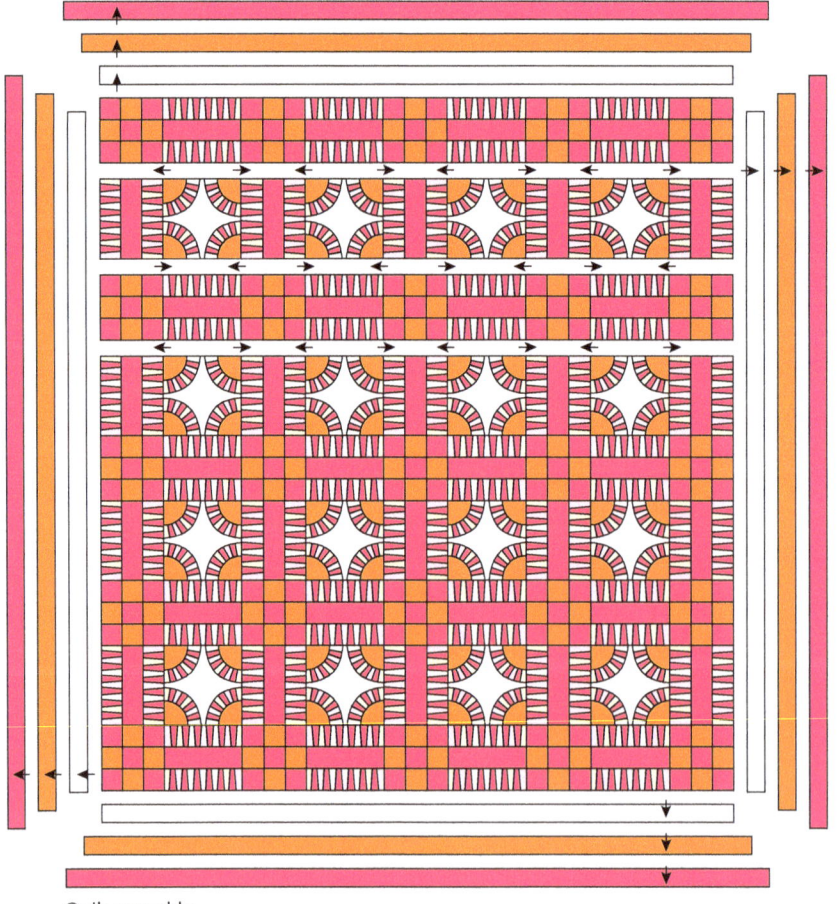

Quilt assembly

SCRAP QUILT SECRETS

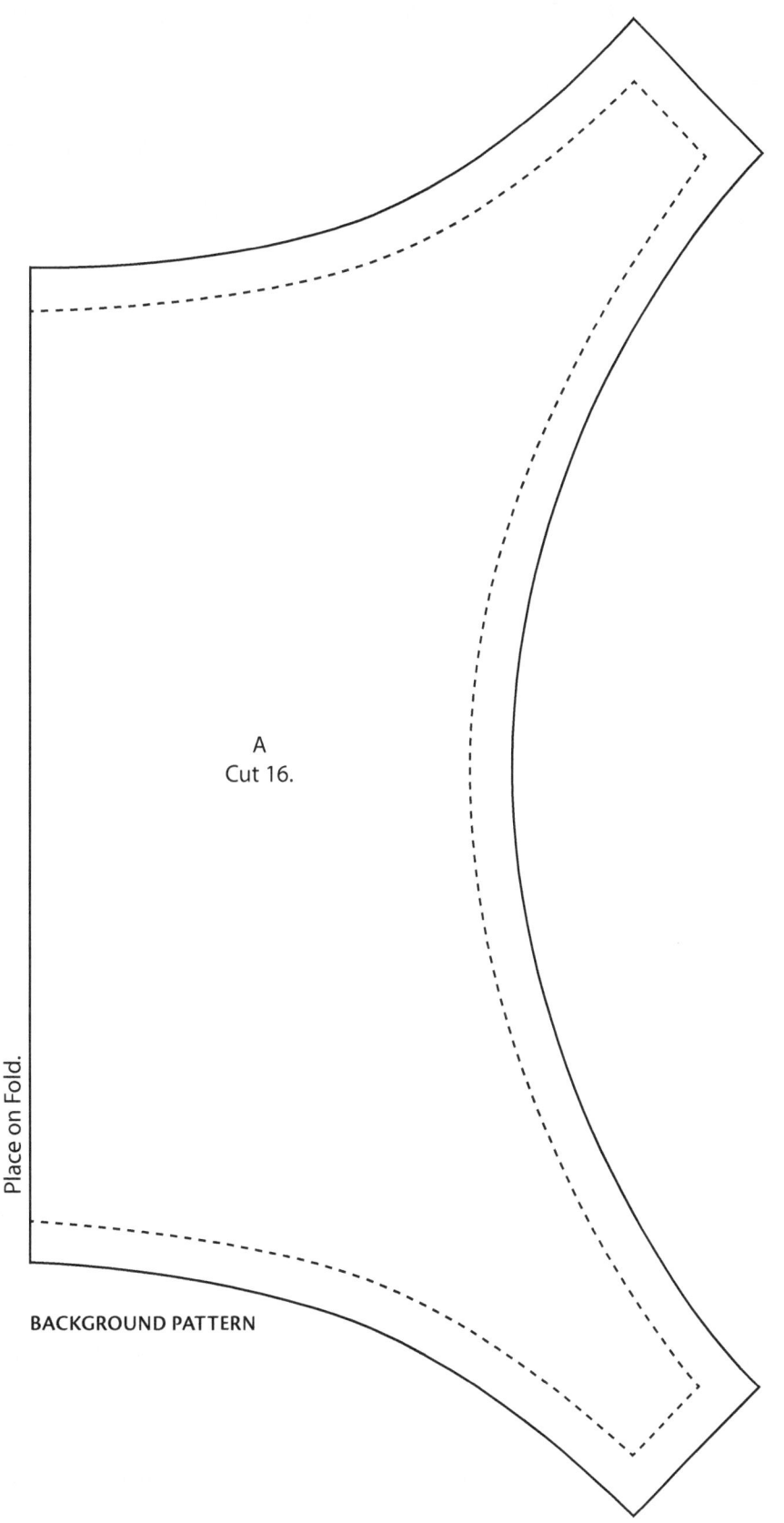

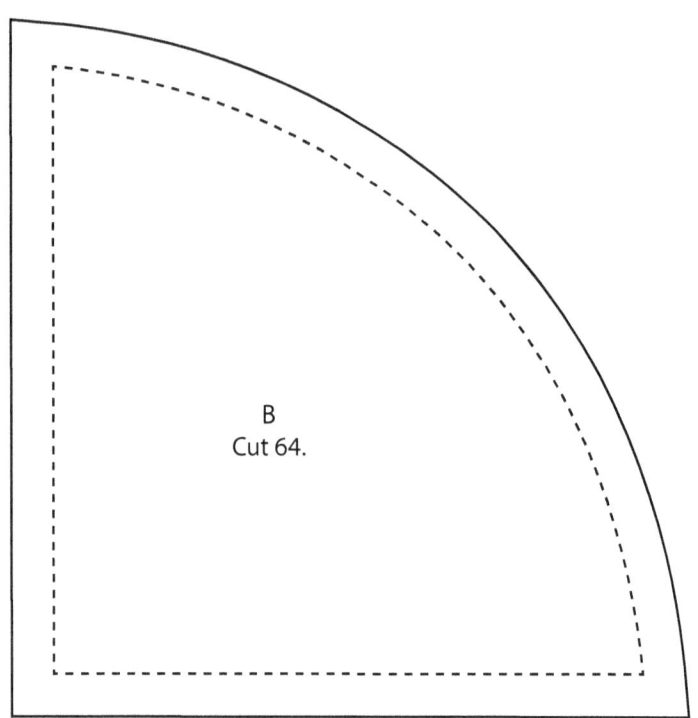

QUARTER-CIRCLE PATTERN

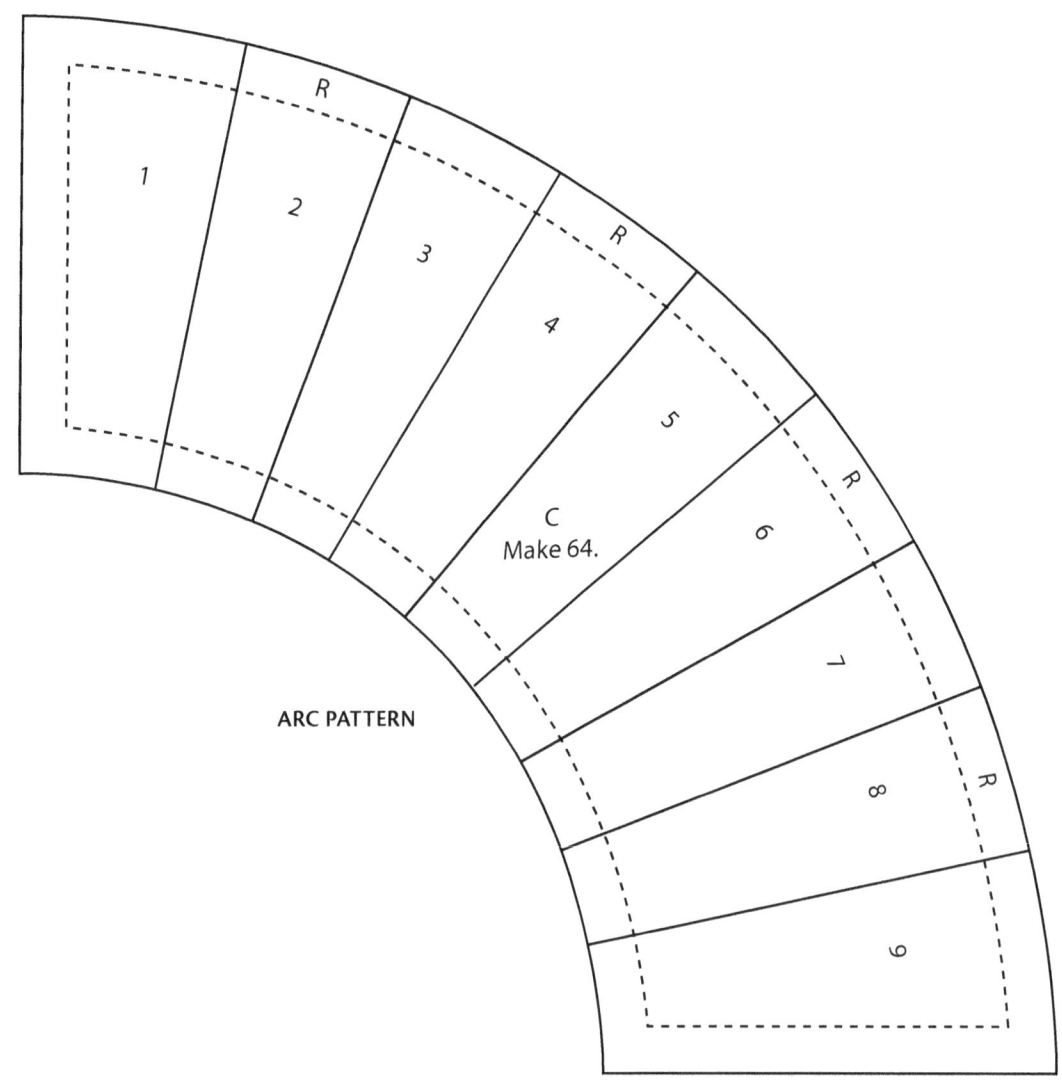

ARC PATTERN

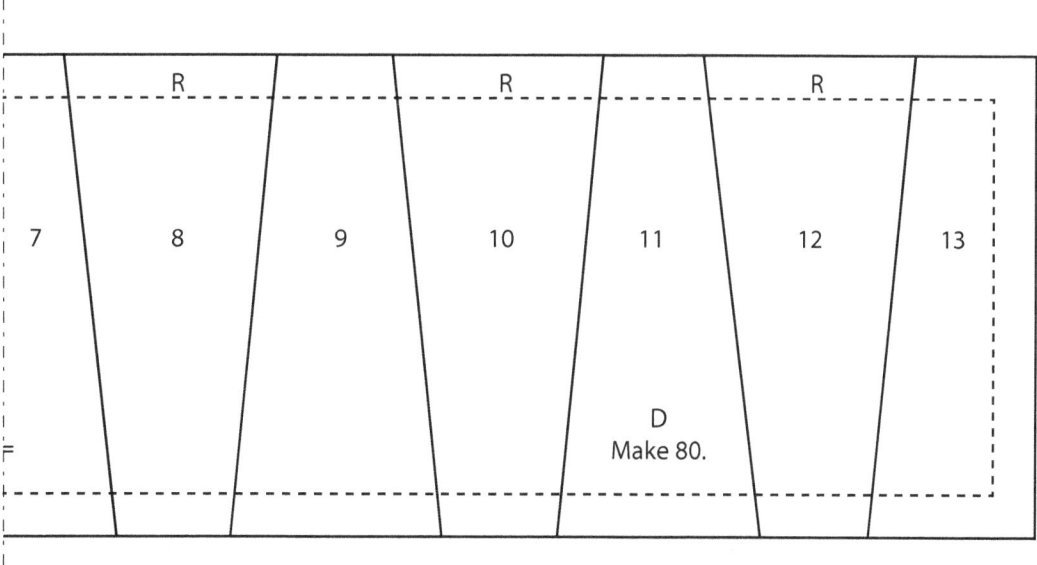

Copy and join the sections to make a master pattern for copying.

SASHING PATTERN

USING Palettes

Before making my first quilt (which was a scrap quilt—a sign of things to come!), I was taught to choose a "magic fabric," also called a "focus fabric," with multiple colors that I liked. Using that fabric as the starting point, you base the entire quilt on colors from that one print. This is a good method, because if you really love the fabric, chances are you are going to love the colors that you collect from that particular color palette.

What happens, however, if you are working from a scrap basket that has no magic fabric? Looking at your stash, you can isolate pieces by lights and darks to establish a palette. You can also choose two colors and pull prints that include those colors to create a specific two-color palette.

Random scraps

Dark palette

Light palette

Two-color palette

Inspiration for a color palette can be found anywhere. I love to look at antique quilts for color combinations. You might also step outside and let nature inspire you. Colors are constantly changing from season to season. Even a favorite photo might become the basis for your palette. By choosing two or three colors and using various shades of those colors, wonderful things can happen. Using a color palette in combination with contrast (page 24) can be extremely effective in achieving a harmonious quilt that will be a favorite for years to come.

USING PALETTES

OH MY STARS

Pieced by Diane D. Knott and quilted by Betty Alonsious

Finished quilt: 90″ × 90″

Finished block: 12″ × 12″

SKILL LEVEL: MODERATE

This quilt was inspired by a block swap with my bee group. We each provided a fabric to be used as a color guide, with stars as a theme. Each person then made a star block in colors that complemented the fabric provided. I designed the featured quilt using the border fabric as my color guide and pieced star blocks similar to the original blocks made by my quilting friends. The light, bright combination of colors looks fresh and cool, but this pattern would also be interesting in patriotic fabrics or a dark palette of solids.

MATERIALS

- **Light scraps:** 3 yards total for blocks
- **Medium scraps in blue, green, lavender, and pink:** 3⅝ yards total for blocks
- **Green fabric:** ⅝ yard for sashing blocks
- **Blue green:** ⅝ yard for sashing blocks and border blocks
- **Blue polka dot:** 2½ yards for sashing and border blocks
- **Focus fabric:** 2¼ yards* for border and binding
- **Backing:** 8¼ yards
- **Batting:** 98″ × 98″

*This yardage assumes lengthwise binding strips. If you want to cut crosswise binding strips, you'll need 3 yards.

Preview Colors

Use a camera to snap photos of color combinations and fabric choices. It's easier to see how the block or quilt will look later by viewing it in a photo. This works when buying fabric as well. Taking a photo of the fabric will show how it will read once it's in the quilt.

CUTTING

All measurements include ¼″-wide seam allowances.

Light scraps
- Cut 25 matching pairs of squares 5¾″ × 5¾″ for star points.
- Cut 9 matching sets of 5 squares 4½″ × 4½″ for block A.
- Cut 4 matching sets of 8 squares 2½″ × 2½″ for block B.
- Cut 4 matching pairs of squares 5¼″ × 5¼″ for block C.
- Cut 8 matching sets of 10 squares 2½″ × 2½″ for block D.

Green fabric
- Cut 18 squares 4¾″ × 4¾″.

Blue green
- Cut 18 squares 4¾″ × 4¾″.
- Cut 2 squares 7¾″ × 7¾″.

Medium scraps
- Cut 25 matching pairs of squares 5¾″ × 5¾″ for star points.
- Cut 9 matching sets of 20 squares 2½″ × 2½″ for block A.
- Cut 4 matching sets of 5 squares 4½″ × 4½″ for block B.
- Cut 4 matching sets for block C as follows:
  2 squares 5¼″ × 5¼″
  1 square 4½″ × 4½″
- Cut 8 matching sets of 10 squares 2½″ × 2½″ for block D.

Blue polka dot
- Cut 6 strips 12½″ × width of fabric; subcut 60 rectangles 3½″ × 12½″.
- Cut 2 squares 7¾″ × 7¾″.

Focus fabric
- Cut 4 strips 6½″ × 78½″.
- Cut 5 strips 2″ × length of fabric for binding.

OH MY STARS

Star Point Assembly

Refer to Quiltmaking Basics (page 93) as needed.

1. Draw a diagonal line from corner to corner on the wrong side of 2 matching light 5¾" squares. Layer the marked squares right sides together with 2 matching medium 5¾" squares. Sew ¼" away on each side of the drawn line. Cut on the line and press the seams toward the darker fabric to make 4 matching half-square triangles.

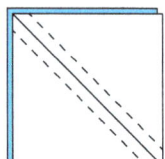 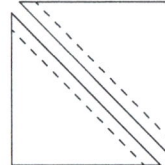 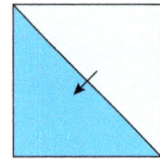 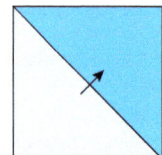

Draw, sew, cut, and press.

2. Layer the units from Step 1 right sides together, with dark facing light and light facing dark. Draw a diagonal line from corner to corner, perpendicular to the seam on the top unit. Sew ¼" away on each side of the drawn line. Cut on the line. Pinwheel-press the seams (page 94) and trim the blocks to 4½" × 4½".

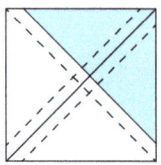 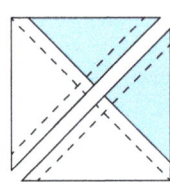 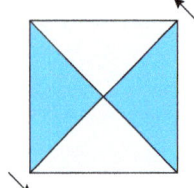 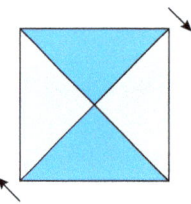

Draw, sew, cut, and press.

3. Repeat with all of the light and medium/dark 5¾" squares to make a total of 25 matching sets of 4 star point units (100 total).

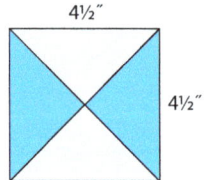

Make 100.

Secrets for Successful Block Swaps

* Choose a block that fits each quilter's skill level.

* Designate a time frame for each step in the swap.

* Be specific about fabric selections and color options.

* Do your best work and respect deadlines.

* Be encouraging of new quilters and offer to help them learn techniques.

* Use blocks that might not be up to your level of work—after all, someone tried her or his best!

* Always remember, friends are more important than fabric!

Star Block A Assembly

For block A, you'll need a set of 20 matching medium 2½" squares, a set of 5 matching light 4½" squares, and 4 matching star point units.

1. Draw a diagonal line from corner to corner on the wrong side of the 2½" squares.

2. Place a marked square on opposite corners of a light 4½" square with right sides together. Sew on the drawn line. Trim away the excess, leaving a ¼" seam allowance. Press the seams toward the corners. Repeat on the remaining 2 corners. Make 5 units.

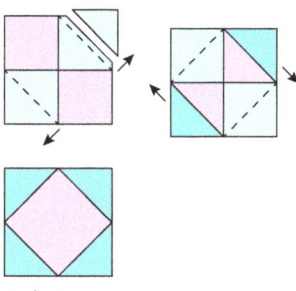

Make 5.

3. Arrange the units from Step 2 with 4 matching star point units in 3 rows as shown. Sew the units into rows. Press the seams away from the star point units. Sew the rows together. Press the seams away from the center row.

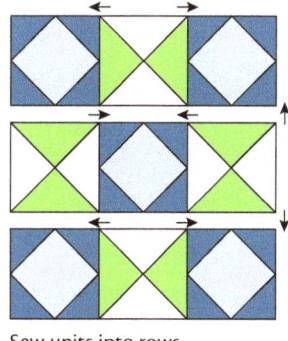

Sew units into rows.

4. Repeat Steps 1–3 to make 9 of Star block A.

Star block A—make 9.

Star Block B Assembly

For block B you'll need a set of 8 matching light 2½" squares, 5 matching medium 4½" squares, and 4 matching star point units.

1. Draw a diagonal line from corner to corner on the wrong side of the 2½" squares.

2. Place 2 marked squares on opposite corners of 4 medium 4½" squares with right sides together. Sew on the drawn line. Trim away the excess, leaving a ¼" seam allowance. Press the seams toward the corners. Make 4 units.

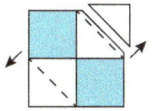 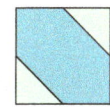

Make 4.

3. Arrange the units from Step 2, the matching 4½" square, and 4 star point units in 3 rows as shown. Sew the units into rows. Press the seams away from the star point units. Sew the rows together. Press the seams away from the center row.

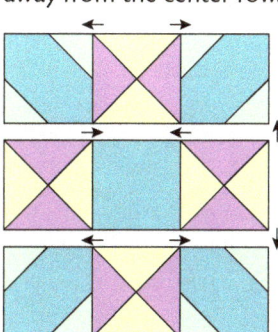

Sew units into rows.

4. Repeat Steps 1–3 to make 4 of Star block B.

Star block B—make 4.

OH MY STARS 73

Star Block C Assembly

For block C you'll need 2 matching light 5¼" squares, a set of 2 matching medium 5¼" squares and 1 matching 4½" square, and 4 matching star point units.

1. Follow Star Point Assembly, Step 1 (page 72), to make 4 half-square triangles using the light and medium 5¼" squares. Press the seams toward the darker side. Trim to 4½" square.

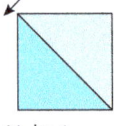
Make 4.

2. Arrange the units from Step 1, the remaining 4½" square, and 4 matching star point units in 3 rows as shown. Sew the units into rows. Press the seams away from the star point units. Sew the rows together. Press the seams away from the center row.

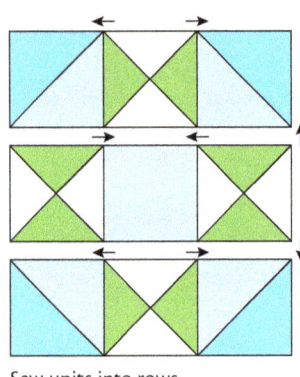
Sew units into rows.

3. Repeat Steps 1 and 2 to make 4 of Star block C.

Star block C—make 4.

Star Block D Assembly

For block D you'll need 10 matching light 2½" squares, 10 matching medium 2½" squares, and 4 star point units.

1. Sew 2 medium 2½" squares and 2 light 2½" squares together in pairs. Press the seams in opposite directions. Sew the 2 units together to make a four-patch. Pinwheel-press the seams (page 94). Make 5.

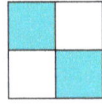
Make 5.

2. Arrange the units from Step 1 and 4 star point units in 3 rows as shown. Sew the units into rows. Press the seams away from the star point units. Sew the rows together. Press the seams away from the center row.

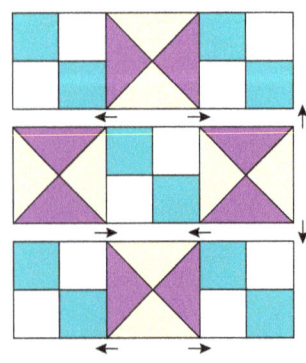
Sew units into rows.

3. Repeat Steps 1 and 2 to make 8 of Star block D.

Star block D—make 8.

Sashing and Border Cornerstone Assembly

1. Follow Star Point Assembly, Steps 1 and 2 (page 72), to make cornerstone blocks using the 4¾" squares of the 2 cornerstone fabrics. Draw the diagonal line on the lighter of the 2 fabrics. Make 36.

2. Trim the blocks to 3½" × 3½".

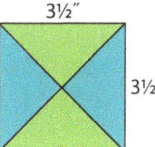

Sashing cornerstone—make 36.

3. Follow Star Point Assembly, Steps 1 and 2, to make cornerstone blocks using the 7¾" squares of cornerstone and sashing fabrics. Draw the diagonal line on the lighter of the 2 fabrics. Make 4.

4. Trim the blocks to 6½" × 6½".

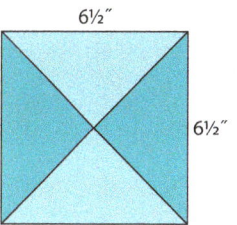

Border cornerstone—make 4.

Quilt Assembly

1. Arrange the blocks, sashing, and cornerstones as shown in the quilt assembly diagram (below right). Note the direction of the diagonal design in the D block. Orient the blocks as shown or as desired.

2. Sew the 6 rows of sashing and cornerstones together. Press the seams toward the sashing.

3. Sew the 5 rows of blocks and sashing together. Press the seams toward the sashing.

4. Sew the rows together. Press the seams toward the sashing and cornerstone rows.

5. Sew a border to the left and right sides of the quilt. Press toward the borders.

6. Sew the border cornerstone blocks onto each end of the 2 remaining borders. Sew these to the top and bottom of the quilt. Press the seams toward the borders.

7. Layer the quilt top, batting, and backing. Baste, quilt as desired, and bind. Refer to Quilt Finishing (page 98) for additional details.

Quilt assembly

VINTAGE VILLAGE

Pieced and quilted by Diane D. Knott

Finished quilt: 68" × 68"

Finished block: 10" × 10"

SKILL LEVEL: EASY

The inspiration for this quilt was a vintage schoolhouse quilt. It had a similar setting, but I chose to make my version with simple house blocks. It's perfect for using up a jelly roll or leftover strips from other projects. I made this quilt for my husband, so I chose a darker, masculine color palette. This pattern would also be fun with brights or neutral prints.

MATERIALS

- **Scraps:** 3¾ yards total
- **Borders and binding:** 2⅝ yards
- **Backing:** 4¼ yards
- **Batting:** 76″ × 76″

Antique Inspiration

Vintage quilts provide interesting patterns and color combinations. Take a closer look at old quilts and find new inspiration for fabric choices, blocks, settings, and quilting designs.

CUTTING

All measurements include ¼″-wide seam allowances.

Scraps for 1 large House block (Cut 20 total.)
- Cut 5 squares 2½″ × 2½″ for sky.
- Cut 1 strip 2½″ × 10½″ for roof.
- Cut 2 squares 2½″ × 2½″ for chimneys.
- Cut 1 strip 2½″ × 4½″ for door.
- Cut 1 square 2½″ × 2½″ for window.
- Cut 1 strip 2½″ × 10½″, 3 strips 2½″ × 4½″, and 1 square 2½″ × 2½″ for walls.

Scraps for 1 small House block (Cut 20 total.)
- Cut 5 squares 1½″ × 1½″ for sky.
- Cut 1 strip 1½″ × 5½″ for roof.
- Cut 2 squares 1½″ × 1½″ for chimneys.
- Cut 1 strip 1½″ × 2½″ for door.
- Cut 1 square 1½″ × 1½″ for window.
- Cut 1 strip 1½″ × 5½″, 3 strips 1½″ × 2½″, and 1 square 1½″ × 1½″ for walls.

Scraps for pieced border
- Cut 112 squares 2½″ × 2½″.

Borders and binding
- Cut 8 strips 2″ × width of fabric for binding.

Then, cut the following on the lengthwise grain:
- Cut 2 strips 2½″ × 50½″.
- Cut 2 strips 2½″ × 54½″.
- Cut 2 strips 5½″ × 58½″.
- Cut 2 strips 5½″ × 68½″.

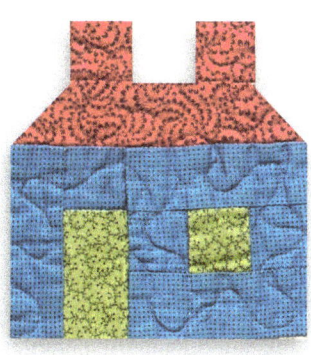

VINTAGE VILLAGE 77

Large House Block Assembly

Refer to Quiltmaking Basics (page 93) as needed.

1. Arrange the pieces for one large block in rows as shown. Note that row 3 is the longest strip of wall fabric and is not pieced.

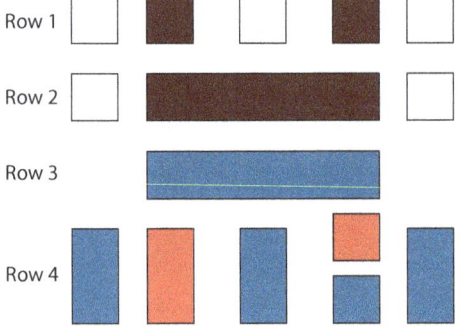

2. For row 1, sew the 3 light squares for the sky and the 2 squares for the chimney together. Press the seams toward the chimney squares.

3. For row 2, draw a diagonal line from corner to corner on the wrong side of 2 squares for the sky. Place the squares right sides together on each end of the roof rectangle. Sew on the marked line, trim the excess fabric, and press the seams toward the sky fabric.

4. For row 4, sew the window square to the wall square. Press the seams toward the wall fabric. Sew together with the 3 wall rectangles and the door rectangle to make row 4. Press the seams toward the wall strips.

5. Sew rows 1–4 together; press the seams as shown. Repeat the steps to make 20 large house blocks.

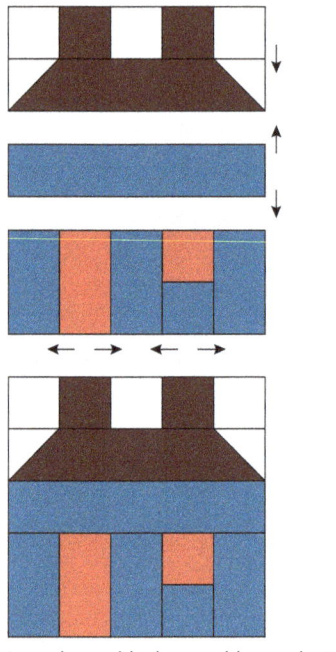

Large house block assembly—make 20.

Small House Block Assembly

1. Follow Large House Block Assembly (above) to make 20 small blocks. In Step 5, you may want to wait to press the row seams until you match up the groups of 4 blocks in the next step. Then press the seams in opposite directions in 2 of the 4 blocks so that the seams will nest together.

2. Sew 4 blocks together to make a large four-patch block. Pinwheel-press the seams (page 94). Make 5 blocks.

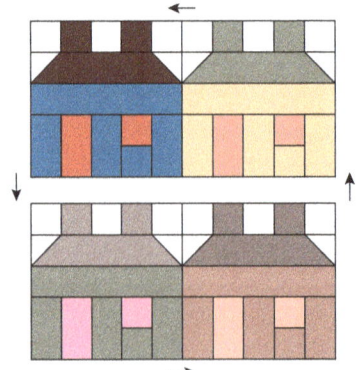

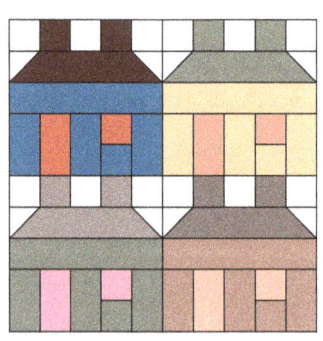

Four-Patch House block assembly—make 5.

Pieced Border Assembly

1. Sew 2 rows of 27 squares, 2½", for the side borders. Press the seams in one direction.

2. Sew 2 rows of 29 squares each for the top and bottom borders. Press the seams in one direction.

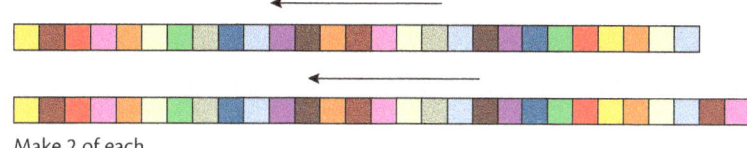

Make 2 of each.

Quilt Assembly

1. Arrange the blocks in 5 rows of 5, according to the quilt assembly diagram (at right). Sew the blocks into rows. Press the rows in alternating directions.

2. Sew the rows together. Press the seams in a single direction.

3. Sew the 2½" × 50½" borders to the left and right sides of the quilt. Press the seams toward the borders.

4. Sew the 2½" × 54½" borders to the top and bottom sides of the quilt. Press the seams toward the borders.

5. Sew the 27-square pieced borders to the left and right sides of the quilt. Press the seams toward the inner borders.

6. Sew the 29-square pieced borders to the top and bottom of the quilt. Press the seams toward the inner borders.

7. Sew the 5½" × 58½" borders to the sides. Press the seams toward the outer borders.

8. Sew the 5½" × 68½" borders to the top and bottom. Press the seams toward the outer borders.

9. Layer the quilt top, batting, and backing. Baste, quilt as desired, and bind. Refer to Quilt Finishing (page 98) for additional details.

Quilt assembly

Have a Little Fun

Note that some blocks have slight variations for added interest. A few houses have only one chimney and some are set against a dark, nighttime sky. This is a design choice, and it's entirely up to you. Each village will be different—make yours uniquely your own!

PEPPERMINT PIE

Pieced by Diane D. Knott and quilted by Betty Alonsious

Finished quilt: 66" × 90"

Finished block: 12" × 12"

SKILL LEVEL: CHALLENGING

Sometimes you want to make a quilt that celebrates a certain holiday, event, or season, but you don't have enough theme fabrics. You can create a holiday palette from almost any scraps! Let your scraps work for you by choosing a very limited palette. By choosing only two or three colors (in this case, reds, greens, and a background), you create the feel of the holiday just as well as any fabric printed specifically for it. Imagine this quilt made from reds, whites, and blues. Immediately, you would have a wonderful patriotic quilt. Or, change the background to black and add batik scraps for an exciting, summery pop of color. Now that you know how this works, combine your scraps in palettes that celebrate anything you choose!

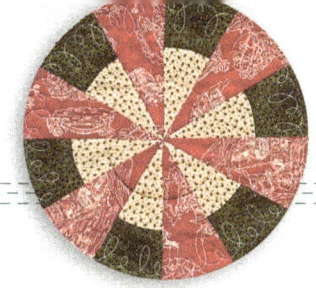

MATERIALS

- **Red scraps:** 2½ yards total
- **Green scraps:** 2 yards total
- **Background:** 5½ yards
- **Backing:** 5½ yards
- **Binding:** ¾ yard
- **Batting:** 74″ × 98″

Seasonal Fabric

When buying fabric, don't let its marketing theme limit you. If a red Christmas print looks perfect for a patriotic quilt, then it will be. Don't be afraid to use a fabric for something other than what it was intended. Color and scale are more important. The background fabric for this quilt was from an autumn-themed fabric line, yet it works just as well in this Christmas palette.

CUTTING

Make templates for pieces A, B, C, and D, using the patterns (pages 86 and 87) and referring to Making and Using Templates (page 96). All measurements include ¼″-wide seam allowances.

Reds
- Cut 22 strips 2″ × 13″.
- Cut 36 squares 2″ × 2″.
- Cut 102 of template A (17 matching sets of 6).

Greens
- Cut 22 strips 2″ × 13″.
- Cut 36 green squares 2″ × 2″.
- Cut 42 of template A (7 matching sets of 6).
- Cut 60 of template C (10 matching sets of 6).

Background
- Cut 12 strips 6½″ × width of fabric. Subcut 68 squares 6½″ × 6½″; from the squares, cut 68 of template D.
- Cut 23 strips 3½″ × width of fabric. Subcut 82 rectangles 3½″ × 6½″. Subcut 72 rectangles 3½″ × 2″. Subcut 14 rectangles 3½″ × 12½″.
- Cut 11 strips 2″ × width of fabric. Subcut 32 strips 2″ × 13″.
- Cut 60 of pattern B.

Binding
- Cut 9 strips 2″ × width of fabric.

Secrets for Saving Time

- *Strip piece the Four-Patch blocks.*
- *Chain piece the units.*
- *Piece the pies using the tips in Sewing Curves (page 50).*
- *Fuse or appliqué the pies on a 12½″ square background, if you prefer.*
- *Make the design work for you by changing any elements you want to avoid.*

PEPPERMINT PIE 81

Four-Patch Block Assembly

Refer to Quiltmaking Basics (page 93) as needed.

1. Sew a red 2″ × 13″ strip to a green 2″ × 13″ strip along the long edges to make a strip set. Press the seams toward the red. Make 6 strip sets. Crosscut the strip sets into 2″ segments for a total of 36.

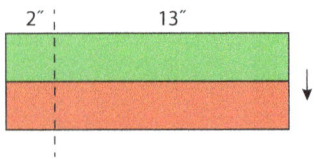

2. Sew 2 segments together into a Four-Patch block. Pinwheel-press the seams (page 94). Make 18 blocks.

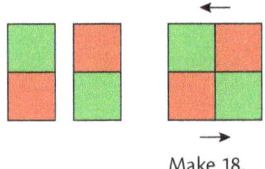

Make 18.

3. Sew a red 2″ × 13″ strip to a background 2″ × 13″ strip to make a strip set. Press the seams toward the red. Make 16 strip sets. Crosscut the strip sets into 2″ segments for a total of 96. Sew the segments into Four-Patch blocks. Pinwheel-press the seams. Make 48 blocks. Set aside 12 for the border.

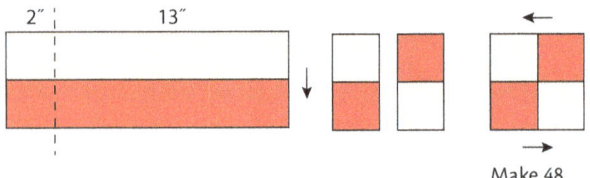

Make 48.

4. Repeat Step 3 to sew a green 2″ × 13″ strip to a background 2″ × 13″ strip to make a strip set. Press the seams toward the green. Make 16 strip sets. Crosscut the strip sets into 2″ segments for a total of 96. Sew the segments into 48 Four-Patch blocks. Set aside 12 for the border.

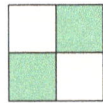

Make 48.

Chain Block Assembly

1. Sew background 2″ × 3½″ rectangles to opposite sides of a red/green Four-Patch block as shown. A red square should be in the upper left corner. Press the seams toward the four-patch. Make 18 of these units.

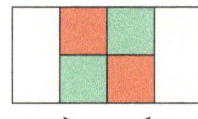

2. Sew a red 2″ square and a green 2″ square to opposite ends of a background 2″ × 3½″ rectangle. Press the seams toward the squares. Make 36 units.

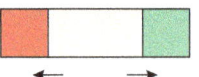

3. Sew a unit from Step 2 to the top and bottom of a unit from Step 1. Position the red and green squares so that they create a red diagonal and a green diagonal. Press the seams away from the four-patch. Make 18.

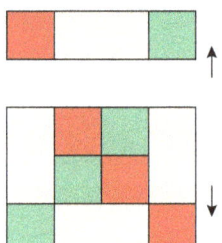

4. Sew a red Four-Patch block to the left end of a 3½″ × 6½″ background rectangle. Sew a green four-patch to the opposite end. Press the seams toward the rectangle. Make 36 units.

SCRAP QUILT SECRETS

5. Sew a 3½″ × 6½″ background rectangle to opposite sides of the units from Step 3. Press the seams toward the rectangles. Sew 2 units from Step 4 to the top and bottom and press the seams away from the center to complete the Chain block. Make 18 blocks.

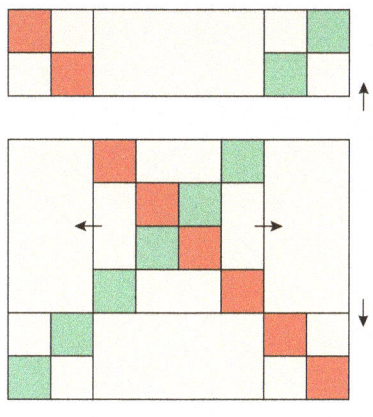

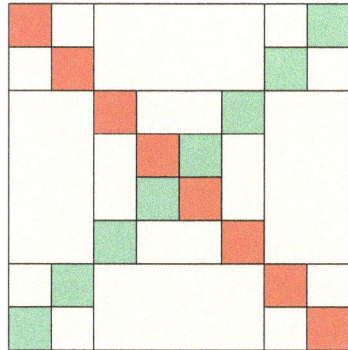

Make 18.

Pie Block Assembly

For each block, you'll need 6 matching red A shapes, 6 matching green A shapes, and 4 background D shapes.

1. Sew the red and green A shapes together in groups of 3 along the long sides, alternating the red and green.

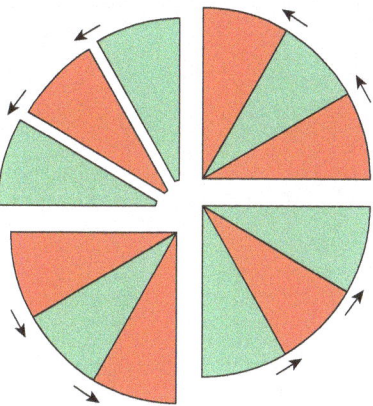

2. Sew a background D piece to each of the wedge units using a curved seam (page 50). Press the seams toward the background. Clip the seam allowance as needed so that the unit lies flat.

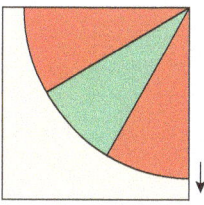

3. Sew the 4 sections together to make the block. Pinwheel-press the seams (page 94). Repeat Steps 1 and 2 to make 7 blocks.

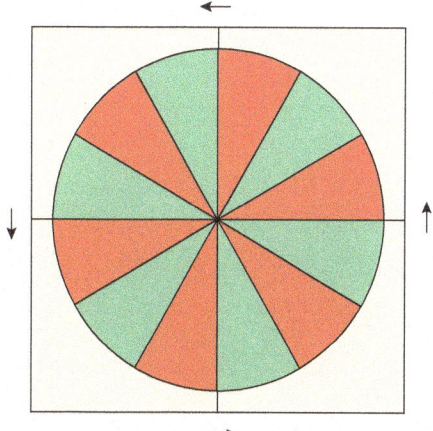

Pie block assembly—make 7.

PEPPERMINT PIE 83

Pie Variation Block Assembly

For each block, you'll need 6 matching red A shapes, 6 background B shapes, 6 matching green C shapes, and 4 background D shapes.

1. Sew a background B piece to a green C piece using a curved seam. Press the seams toward the background. Make 6 units.

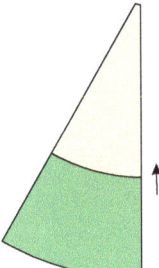

Make 6.

2. Repeat Pie Block Assembly, Steps 1 and 2, to sew the B/C units to the red A pieces and complete the block. Make 10 blocks.

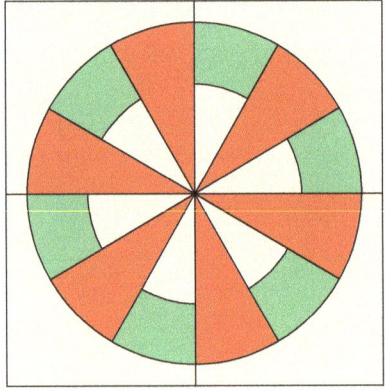

Pie variation block—make 10.

Border Block Assembly

1. Sew a red Four-Patch block and a green Four-Patch block on opposite ends of a 3½" × 6½" background rectangle. Be sure to orient the blocks as shown. Press the seams toward the rectangle. Make 4 border blocks with the red four-patch on the left and 6 with the red four-patch on the right for a total of 10 border blocks.

Make 4.

Make 6.

2. Set aside the 4 remaining Four-Patch blocks for use in the quilt assembly.

84 SCRAP QUILT SECRETS

Quilt Assembly

1. Arrange the Pie blocks and the Chain blocks into 7 rows of 5 blocks in each, alternating the blocks. Orient the Chain blocks so that the green and red squares create the diagonal chains across the quilt. Add the border blocks and the 3½˝ × 12½˝ background rectangles to the sides, top, and bottom. Add the remaining Four-Patch blocks to the corners.

2. Sew the blocks into rows and press the seams toward the Pie blocks. Sew the rows together; press the seams in one direction.

3. Layer the quilt top, batting, and backing. Baste, quilt as desired, and bind. Refer to Quilt Finishing (page 98) for additional details.

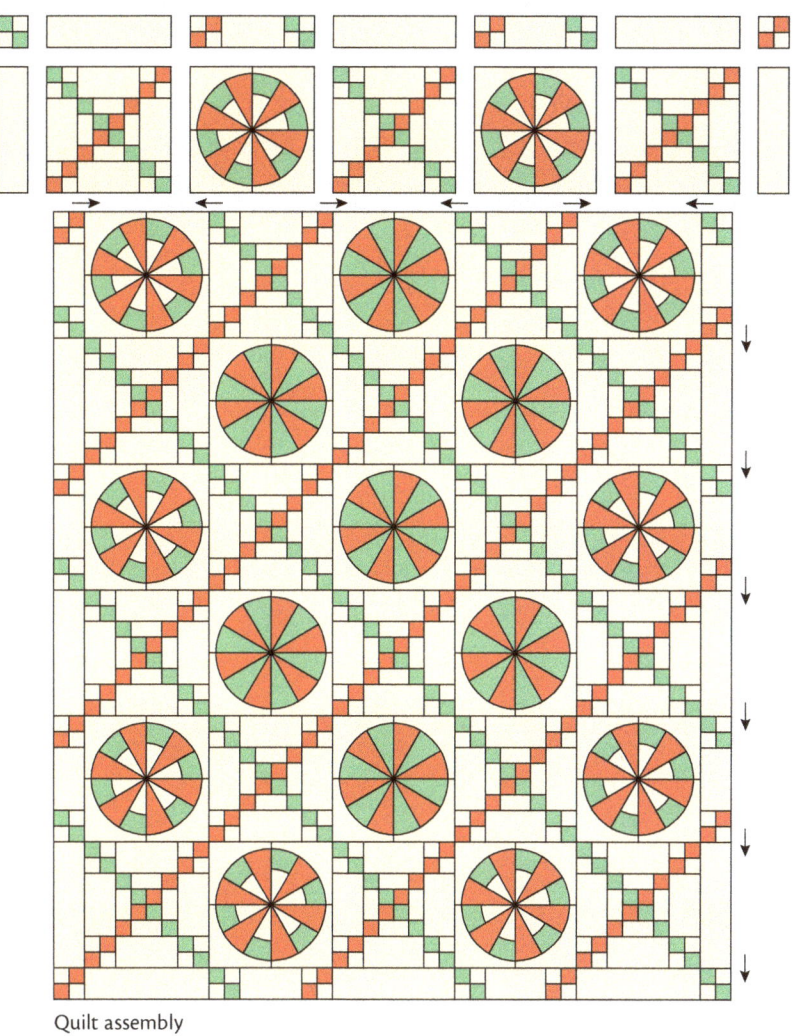

Quilt assembly

PEPPERMINT PIE 85

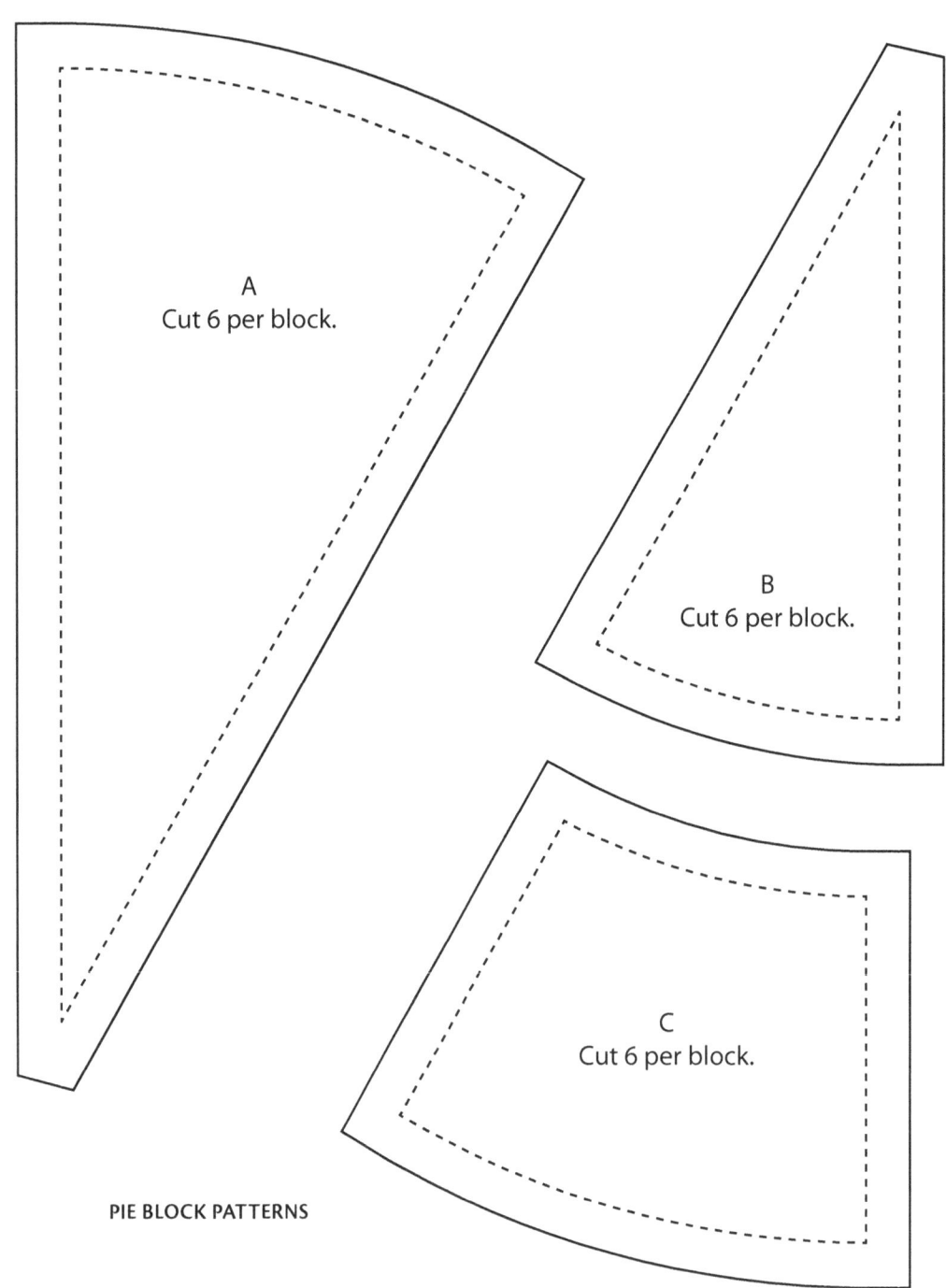

PIE BLOCK PATTERNS

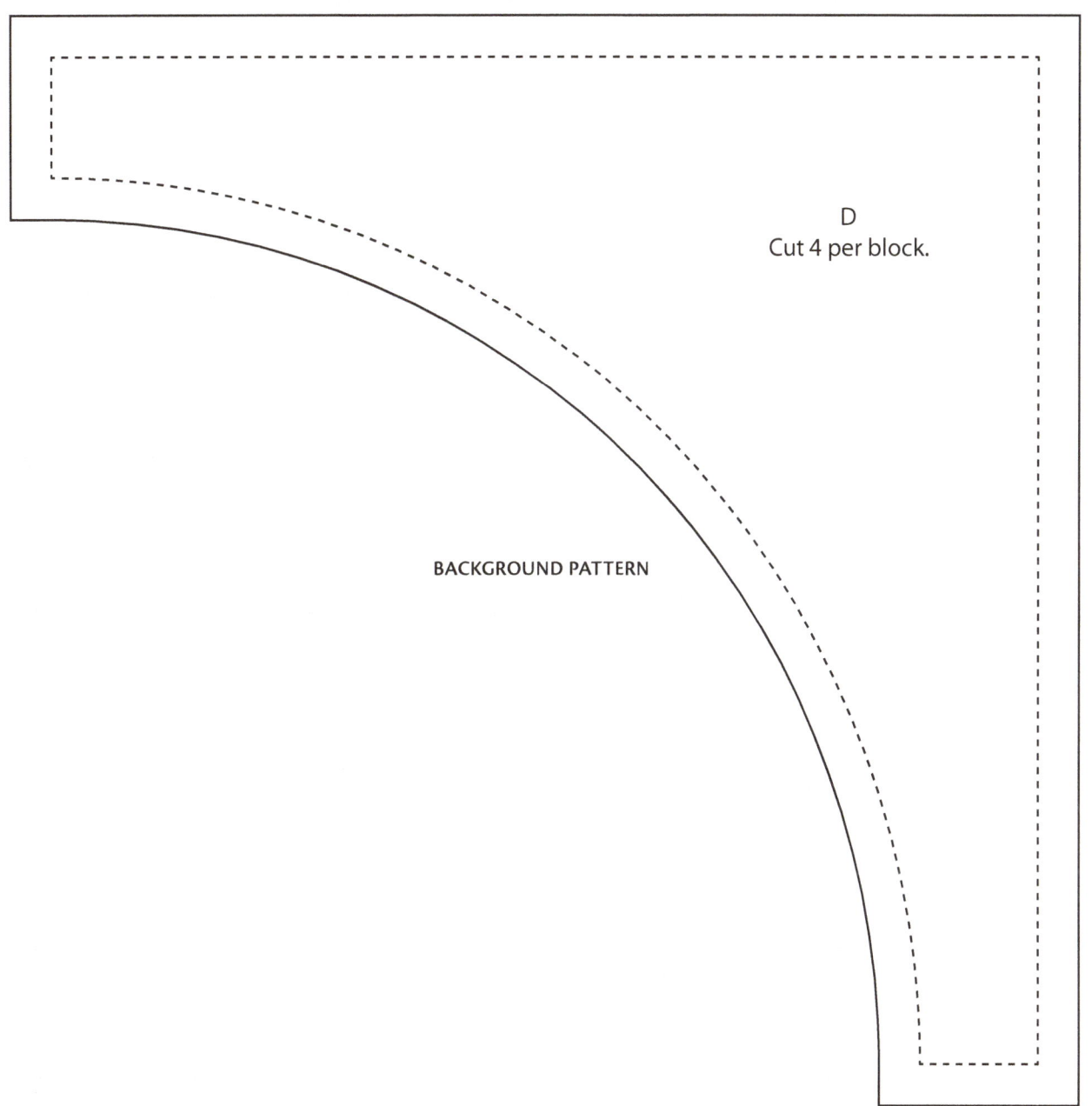

D
Cut 4 per block.

BACKGROUND PATTERN

Pattern Tip

When making templates from freezer paper, press 3 or 4 layers of freezer paper together to form a stiff, thicker pattern. This will reduce shifting and increase accuracy.

PEPPERMINT PIE

USING *Selvages*

Selvages

Selvages are the lengthwise edges of the fabric as it comes off the bolt. The selvage is usually less than 1″ wide and contains written information from the manufacturer, such as the designer, the line of fabric, and the colors used in the printing process. It is also a closer, tighter weave than the body of the fabric. Many times the selvage will be thicker than the rest of the fabric and sometimes it contains little frayed pieces of thread. For these reasons, the selvages are typically cut away and discarded before using the fabric.

Why Use Selvages?

For scrap quilters, the idea of throwing away any part of the fabric gives us pause. Besides, so many selvages are really fascinating because of the lettering and tiny color palettes. It's easy enough to toss them all into a basket or bin and save them for later. The variety of prints and styles makes a quilt more interesting and adds a punch of color. Of course, you can use selvages in other items as well as quilts.

How to Sew Selvages

Selvages are top-stitched to one another. Layer one selvage over another with a ¼″ overlap. Both selvages will be right sides up. Topstitch them together along the bound edge of the selvage that is layered on top. The raw edge of the selvage on bottom will be hidden in the seam allowance. Repeat this process until the size of unit needed is reached. Press the selvages flat both before and after sewing.

Arrange selvages next to machine.

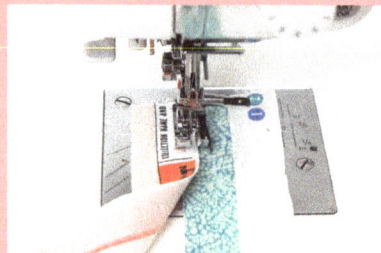
Topstitch together.

Secrets for Working with Selvages

* When cutting, always leave a minimum of ¼″ of fabric next to the selvage for your seam allowance.

* Vary the cutting width of the selvages from 1¼″ to 2½″ for more interest.

* Choose a color thread that will match most of your selvages because the stitching will show on the front of the quilt.

* Cut long selvages into usable lengths to avoid tangling; I cut mine 18″–24″ long.

* Selvages will lie flat and be easier to work with if they have been pressed.

* If you need more selvages, just ask your quilting friends. You will be amazed how many little baggies of selvages start appearing! Once word got out that I was using selvages, people started mailing them to me, giving them to me at meetings, and dropping them in my tote bag when I wasn't even looking.

GIFT BASKETS

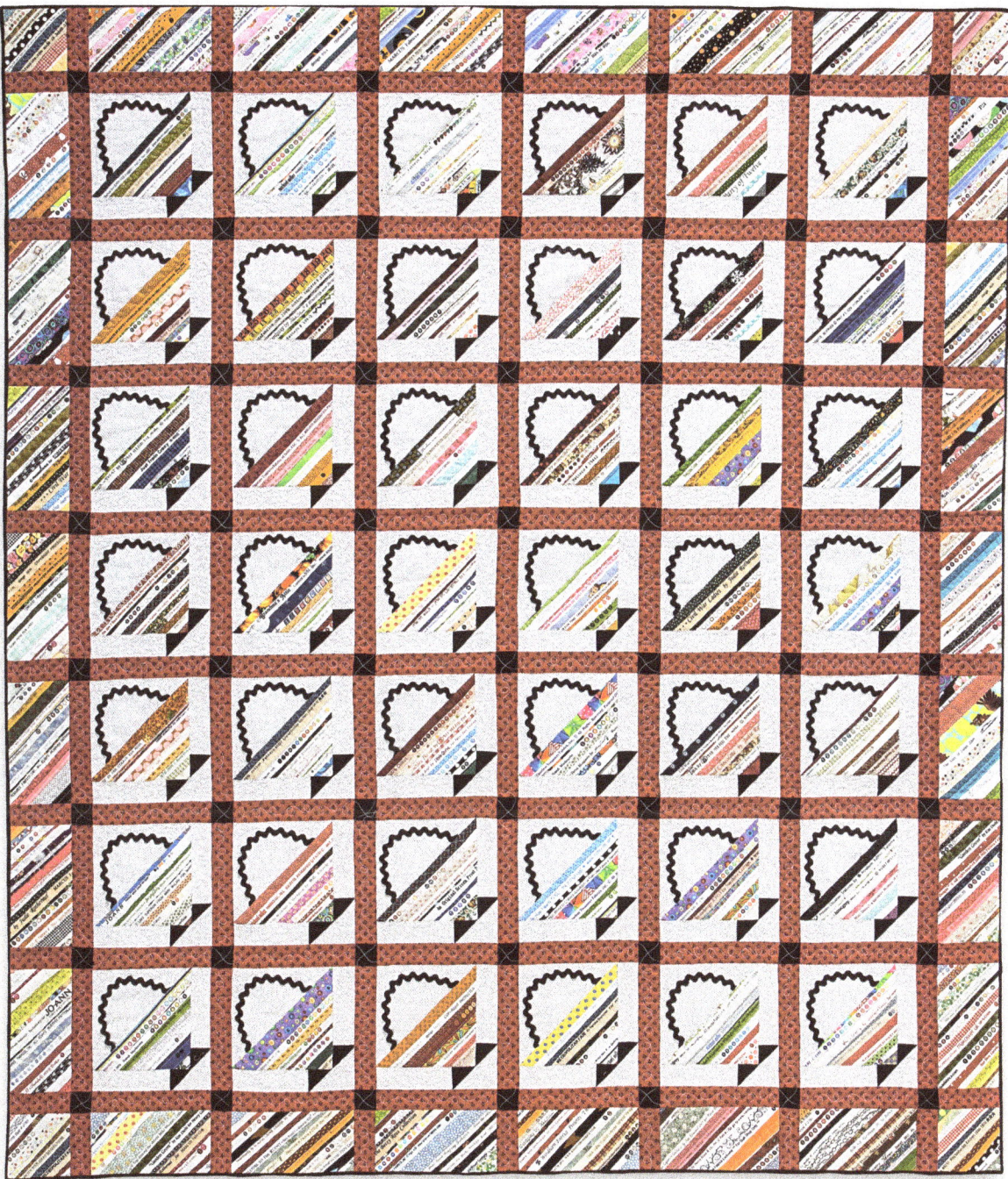

Pieced by Diane D. Knott and quilted by Betty Alonsious

Finished quilt: 70″ × 80″

Finished block: 8½″ × 8½″

SKILL LEVEL: EASY

Selvage quilts can be addictive. Once you make your first, you will start looking at selvages with much more interest. Any quilt block can be converted to a selvage block, piecing selvage strips. I chose a classic Basket block to use selvages, but other classic blocks work well, too.

GIFT BASKETS

MATERIALS

- **Selvages:** Approximately 135 yards*
- **Black fabric:** ½ yard
- **Red fabric:** 1¾ yards
- **Background:** 2¼ yards
- **Rickrack:** 12 yards, ⅝" wide
- **Backing:** 5 yards
- **Binding:** ⅔ yard
- **Batting:** 78" × 88"

*This amount is based on selvage strips cut with ¼" extra for seam allowance. You'll need less if your strips are wider. The total amount needed will vary greatly depending on the width of your strips. I usually tell students that they will need a 20-gallon plastic bin stuffed full!

CUTTING

All measurements include ¼"-wide seam allowances.

Black
- Cut 42 squares 2⅜" × 2⅜"; cut in half on the diagonal.
- Cut 56 squares 2" × 2".

Red
- Cut 25 strips 2" × width of fabric; subcut 97 strips 2" × 9".
- Cut 4 strips 2" × width of fabric; subcut 30 strips 2" × 4¾".

Background
- Cut 5 strips 8" × width of fabric; subcut 21 squares 8" × 8" and cut in half diagonally.
- Cut 2 strips 4" × width of fabric; subcut 21 squares 4" × 4" and cut in half diagonally.
- Cut 14 strips 2" × width of fabric; subcut 84 rectangles 2" × 6".

Rickrack
- Cut 42 pieces 10" long.

Binding
- Cut 8 strips 2" × width of fabric.

Block Assembly

Refer to How to Sew Selvages (page 88) when sewing the selvage strips; refer to Quiltmaking Basics (page 93) as needed.

1. Make a handle placement guide by tracing the pattern (page 92) onto freezer paper, paper, card stock, or template plastic.

2. Fold an 8" background half-square triangle in half to find the center of the long side and finger-press to make a crease. Align the center of the placement guide with the crease and trace lightly around the guide with a pencil. Arrange the rickrack on the drawn line and pin or baste in place. Topstitch the rickrack by machine or appliqué it by hand. Make 42.

3. Sew selvage strips together, beginning with strips that are about 12" long. Add gradually shorter strips until you have a piece big enough to create an 8" half-square triangle (the same size as the background with handle). Use a square ruler at least 9" × 9" (or a 45° triangle ruler) to trim the piece to size. Make 42 triangles.

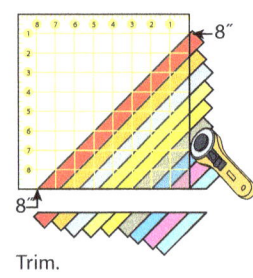

Sew selvages. Trim. Make 42.

4. Sew a selvage triangle to a handle triangle. Press the seams toward the selvage. Trim to 7½" × 7½". Make 42.

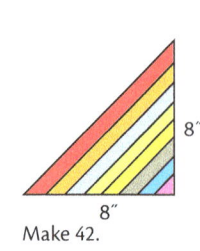

Sew and trim.

5. Sew a black 2⅜" half-square triangle onto the end of a 2" × 6" background rectangle as shown. Repeat to make 42 with the triangles facing left and 42 with the triangles facing right. Press the seams toward the rectangles.

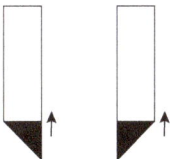

Make 42 of each.

6. Sew a Step 5 unit to each side of the Step 4 basket units. Press the seams toward the rectangles.

7. Sew the background 4" half-square triangle to the black triangles to complete the block. Press the seams toward the background and trim so that the block measures 9" × 9". Make 42 Basket blocks.

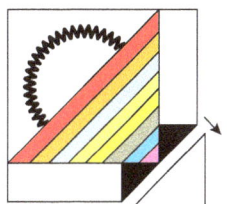

Basket block—make 42.

 **tip**

You can also use foundation piecing when sewing the selvage portion of the basket blocks and border blocks. Trim copy paper, foundation paper, or old phone book pages to the size needed. Sew the selvages to the paper as directed using a shorter than normal stitch length. Trim to the correct size and then carefully remove the paper.

Border Block Assembly

1. Sew selvage strips together, beginning with a strip about 3" long and a strip about 4" long. Add gradually longer and then shorter strips in a staggered manner until you have a piece big enough to cut a 4¾" × 9" rectangle. Use a ruler and rotary cutter to trim the piece to size, aligning the 45° line of the ruler with the edge of one of the selvage strips. Trim 2 sides and then rotate the piece 180° to trim the remaining 2 sides. Make 26 border blocks.

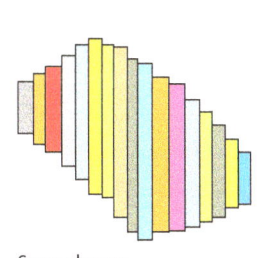
Sew selvages.

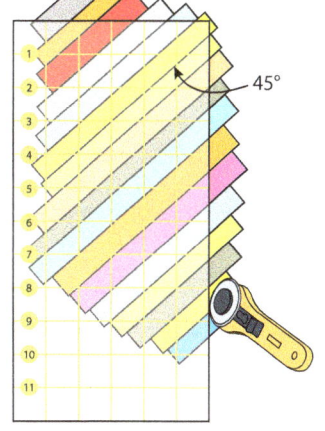
Trim.

Make 26.

2. Repeat Step 1 to create a piece big enough to cut a 4¾" square. Make 4 squares for the border corners.

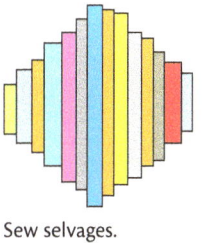
Sew selvages.

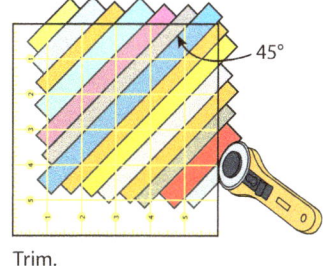
Trim.

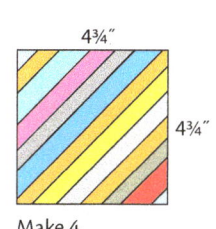
Make 4.

GIFT BASKETS 91

Quilt Assembly

1. Sew the Basket blocks, sashing, and border blocks into rows as shown in the quilt assembly diagram. Press the seams toward the sashing.

2. Sew the rows together. Press the seams toward the sashing rows.

3. Layer the quilt top, batting, and backing. Baste, quilt as desired, and bind. Refer to Quilt Finishing (page 98) for additional details.

> **tip**
>
> **Quilting Selvages**
>
> *Machine quilting is best for quilts containing a lot of selvages. Quilt parallel to the strips so that the stitching doesn't cross over words and numbers.*

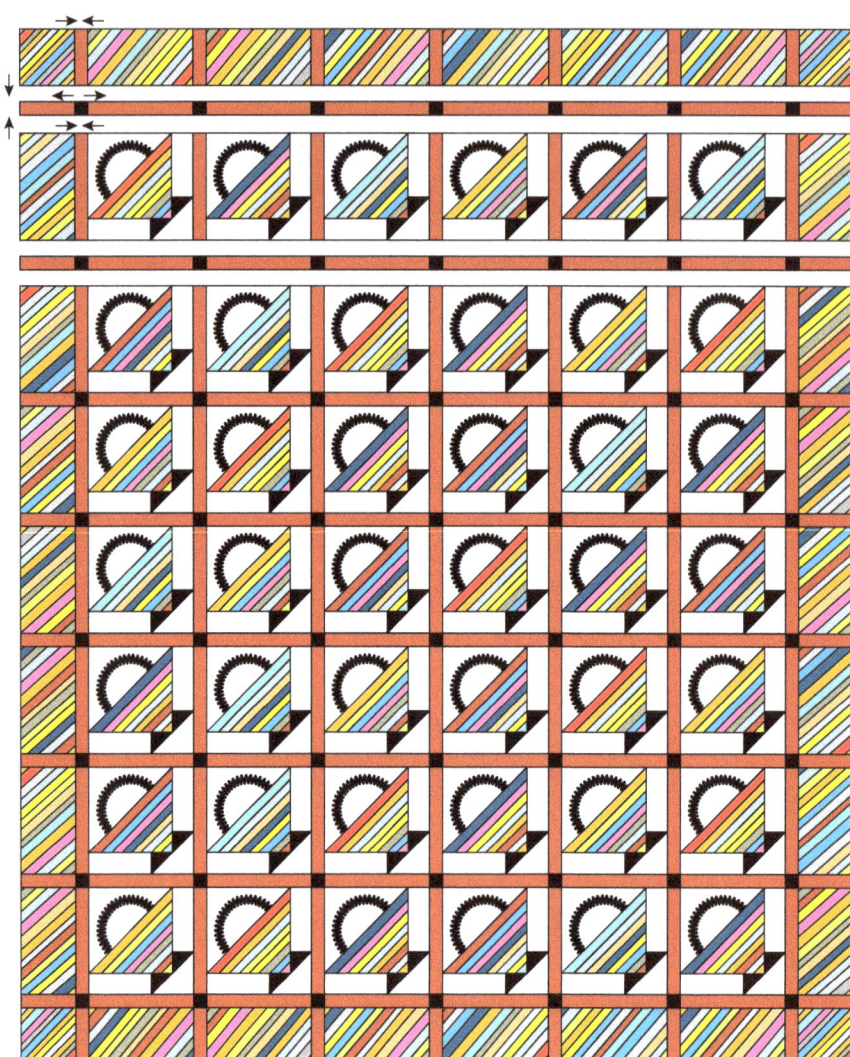

Quilt assembly

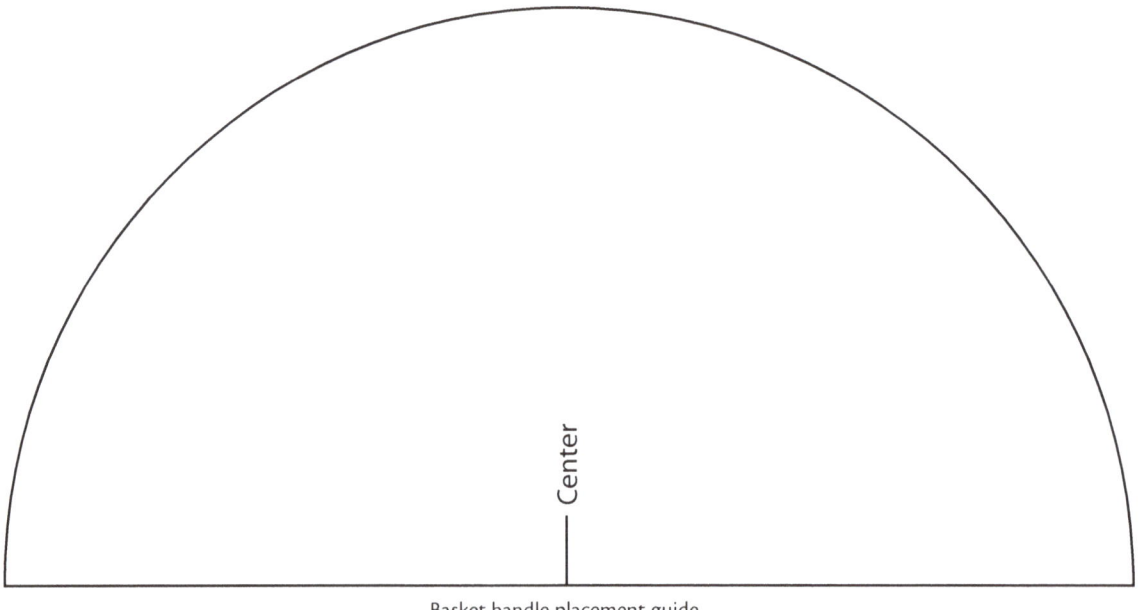

Basket handle placement guide

Quiltmaking BASICS

Supplies

The following are the basic supplies you need to make the quilts in this book:

Basic quilting supplies

- Rotary mat, acrylic rulers, rotary cutter
- Fabric scissors, paper scissors
- Sewing machine
- Iron
- Wooden seam-pressing tool
- Hand and machine needles
- Cotton thread, perle cotton thread
- Thimble for hand sewing
- Seam ripper
- Freezer paper
- Marking pens and pencils
- Binding clips
- Quilter's safety pins
- Add-A-Quarter ruler (*optional*)

Design Surface

Having a large design area is important when making fabric choices or arranging quilt blocks. Whether it's a wall, a table, or even a floor, arranging your choices to view them all at once will help you see the result before actually sewing it all together.

You can buy one of the many design products on the market or simply cover a large board or portion of a wall with felt or flannel, which allows you to place fabric pieces on the surface without pinning. Larger patchwork can be pinned and easily rearranged as needed.

Step back as you are working and making decisions. Taking photos is a good way to see the quilt as you would from a distance. Having photos also allows you to make changes while knowing you can go back to an earlier design if you want. When you are ready to start assembling, take a final photo so you can make sure you get all the pieces in the proper places.

Rotary Cutting

Always press scraps and other fabric flat before cutting them to size with a ruler and rotary cutter. If scraps are large enough, cut strips first, then crosscut the strips to save time and reduce waste.

- Change the blade often for a clean cut the first time.
- Move the fabric or the entire cutting mat so that you always cut away from yourself.
- If you will be sewing pieces right sides together after cutting, cut them with the right sides layered together to reduce handling. This will save time and prevent errors.

Sewing

Always use a ¼" seam allowance for stitching. There are a number of ways to do this.

- Use the edge of a ¼" presser foot.
- Adjust the position of the needle on your machine and use the edge of a standard presser foot.
- Use the fast2sew Ultimate Seam Guide (by C&T Publishing; see Resources, page 111).
- Measure and mark a ¼" seam on your sewing machine.

Use tape to mark exact ¼" seam on your machine.

 tip

Additional Sewing Machines?

If you have more than one machine, be sure to check and mark all of them. Very small differences will add up quickly!

Pressing

Pressing is critical for accuracy. Here are suggestions for best results.

- Use a light touch with a very hot iron (cotton setting). To prevent stretching the fabric, lift and press—do not push, slide, or drag the iron.
- Use a spray bottle of water or a pressing product rather than using water in your iron—your iron will last longer and you will avoid any unpleasant leaking or dripping.
- Always press from the wrong side first to ensure the seams are going in the correct direction. Then turn the patchwork over and press from the front.
- Use an ironing board cover that has straight lines on it. You can use them as a guide to prevent unwanted curves.

tips

Pinwheel Press

This is a great technique to reduce bulk when four seams come together. It's sometimes referred to as "spinning" the seams. I use it when sewing Four-Patch blocks and when joining any four blocks or units together.

1. *Feed the pieced units into the machine with the seam allowance on top facing toward the needle and the seam allowance on the bottom facing the opposite direction.*

2. *Sew the seam, clip the threads, and remove the block from the machine.*

3. *Remove the stitching in the seam allowance of the long seam by **very gently** opening the seam. This will distribute the bulk across the seam intersection.*

4. *Press the seams open in the center. Press the adjacent seams to the side in opposite directions. You'll create a small "four patch" in the center of the block.*

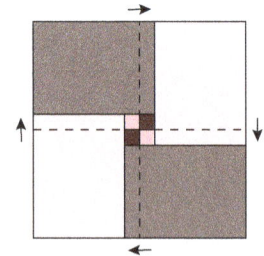

Making Half-Square Triangles

USING SQUARES

1. Cut squares the size indicated in the project instructions. The squares are cut 1¼" larger than the desired finished size so that they can be squared up and trimmed to the exact size needed.

2. Layer 2 squares, right sides together. Draw a diagonal line from corner to corner on the wrong side of the lighter square.

Draw line.

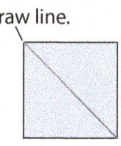

3. Sew a seam ¼" away from the drawn line on both sides. Cut on the drawn line.

4. Open and press. I like to press the seams open, but press toward the darker fabric if you prefer. Trim the units as directed—½" larger than the desired finished size. Your half-square triangles will be perfect!

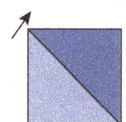

USING STRIPS

I usually cut triangles from strips with a 45° triangle ruler. This saves time and eliminates wasted fabric.

1. Cut strips the size indicated in the instructions. The strip width will be ½" larger than the finished unit. For example, if the finished unit is 2", cut strips 2½" wide.

2. Layer a light and dark fabric strip right sides together.

3. Make a straight cut on one end, and then place the straight edge of your 45° ruler on the cut edge. Cut triangles as shown, aligning the ¼" line of the ruler point with the raw edge of the strip. Rotate the ruler for the next cut. Continue cutting triangles until you have the number needed.

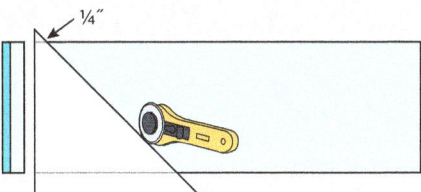

Layer strips right sides together and cut triangles.

4. Sew the triangles together without taking them apart or pinning. Press the seams open.

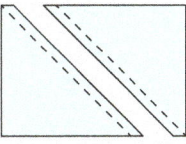 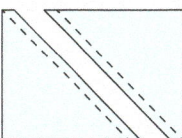

Sew.

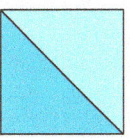 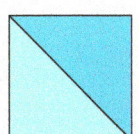 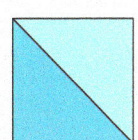 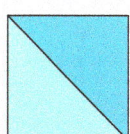

Press.

Making and Using Templates

You will need to make templates for the appliqué patterns and for some of the piecing in this book.
I use freezer paper, but you can also use template plastic or other materials such as card stock if you prefer.

FREEZER PAPER

1. Trace the patterns onto the dull side of a piece of freezer paper with a permanent marker.

2. Press the freezer paper onto 3 or 4 more layers of freezer paper to make a thick, sturdy template.

3. Cut out the shape on the drawn lines using sharp paper scissors.

4. Iron the template onto the right side of the fabric. Cut around it using fabric scissors. You can use a ruler and rotary cutter on top of the template for straight edges if you prefer.

5. After the fabric is cut, carefully peel off the template. The template can be reused many times. Peel off the bottom layer of freezer paper when it no longer adheres to the fabric, and continue using it until the next layer no longer adheres.

TEMPLATE PLASTIC

1. Trace the pattern onto template plastic with a permanent marker and cut it out with scissors.

2. Draw around the shape on the right side of the fabric and cut with scissors, or cut straight edges with a ruler and rotary cutter.

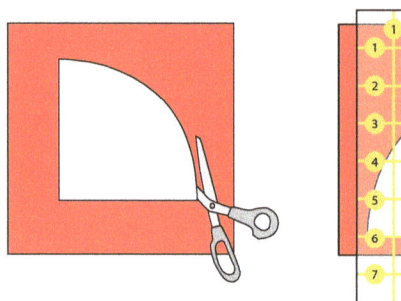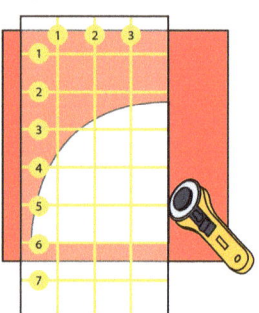

Cut around freezer paper.

Appliqué

You can use any method of appliqué for the projects in this book. The patterns are symmetrical, so there is no need to reverse them for fusible appliqué.

FUSIBLE APPLIQUÉ

When using a fusible product, follow the manufacturer's instructions.

1. Trace the shapes onto the paper side of the fusible web.

2. Fuse the shapes to the wrong side of the appliqué fabric.

3. Cut out the shapes and, if using a paper-backed product, peel off the backing.

4. Place the shapes on the background as shown in the project diagrams and fuse in position.

5. Finish the appliqué edges by hand or by machine, using a zigzag, blanket, or straight stitch.

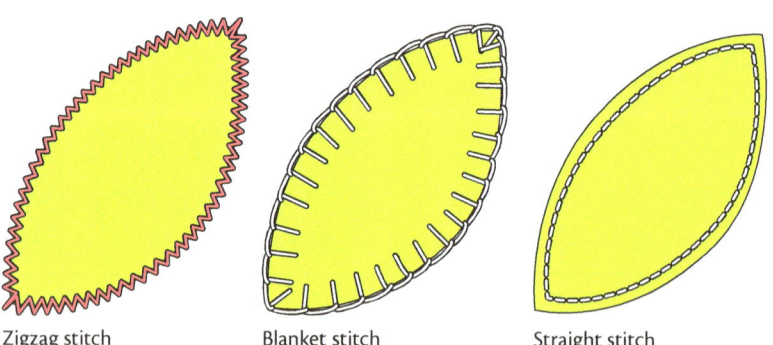

Zigzag stitch   Blanket stitch   Straight stitch

SCRAP QUILT SECRETS

HAND APPLIQUÉ

For hand appliqué, make templates using freezer paper as instructed in Making and Using Templates (page 96).

1. Trace the patterns onto the dull side of the freezer paper. Use just 1 layer of freezer paper.

2. Cut out the drawn shapes on the traced line and press the shiny side of the patterns to the wrong side of the appliqué fabric.

3. Cut the shape from the fabric, adding a scant ¼" seam allowance.

4. Finger press the seam allowance to the wrong side of the applique. Pin the appliqué in place, and stitch by hand, turning the seam allowances under with your needle as you stitch. The finger-pressed crease will help make it easy to turn the fabric under.

5. Remove the freezer paper before taking the last few stitches.

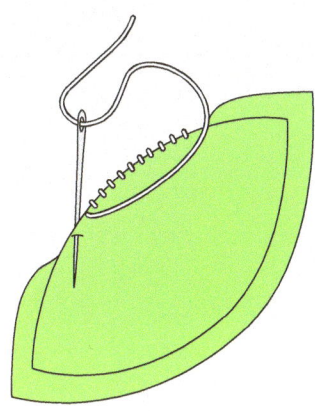

Needle-turn hand appliqué

> **tip**
>
> **Use Cookie Cutters for Appliqué Shapes**
>
> *Cookie cutters are great for making appliqué shapes. Simply trace the design onto paper and cut out the pattern. The shape can be easily resized using a copier after it has been traced.*

WOOL APPLIQUÉ

Felted wool is easy to work with. The edges do not fray, so they do not need to be turned under. Make templates using freezer paper.

1. Trace the patterns onto the dull side of the freezer paper.

2. Cut out the drawn shapes on the traced line and press the shiny side of the patterns to the wool. (Wool is usually the same on both sides.) Cut the shape and remove the freezer paper.

3. Pin or baste the shapes in place on the background.

4. Stitch the shapes in place by hand using a whipstitch or blanket stitch or by machine using a blanket stitch.

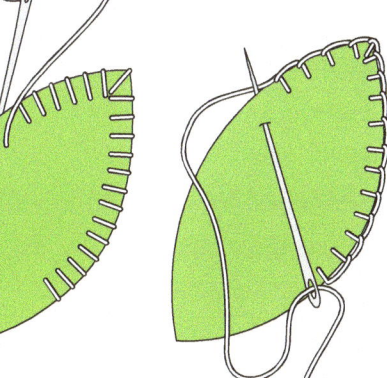

Whipstitch

Blanket stitch

> **tip**
>
> **Matching or Contrasting Thread?**
>
> *With wool appliqué, use a matching thread if you want the stitches to disappear; use a contrasting thread if you want the stitches to stand out.*

BIAS STEMS

Bias stems or vines are easy to make and will curve easily.

1. Cut strips 1¼" wide at a 45° angle to the selvages.

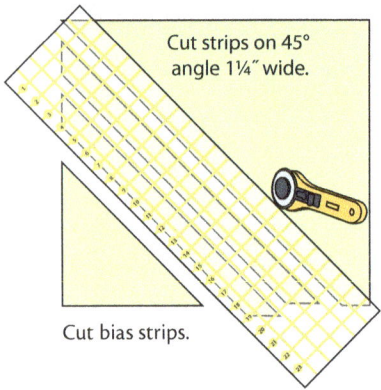
Cut bias strips.

2. Piece the strips, offsetting them by ¼" as shown, and press the seams open.

3. Fold the strip approximately in thirds, folding the edges toward the center and overlapping them, but not all the way. Press the strip flat. The vine should be ½" wide.

4. With the raw edge facing down, place the bias strips on the background according to the pattern directions and pin or baste in place. Stitch by hand or machine.

Sew together.

Press in thirds.

Quilt Finishing

BACKING

Quilt backings can be as creative as the front of the quilt. If you plan to hand quilt, a simple backing with the fewest seams will make that process easier. If you plan to machine quilt, piecing a backing can be fun and economical and adds a nice surprise when the quilt is turned over.

If your backing fabric isn't quite wide enough or long enough, add leftover strips or blocks as needed. You can even piece together something special, just for the back. Add the pieced strip 8"–12" from the top of the quilt. This will be revealed when the top of the quilt is turned back on the bed. It will give the person sleeping under the quilt one last sweet detail to dream about!

Patchwork backing surprise

BASTING

For machine quilting on a domestic machine, pin baste the quilt top, batting, and backing together using quilter's safety pins.

1. Place the quilt backing wrong side up on a table or large flat area.

2. Tape the fabric to the flat surface securely around the edges pulling the fabric smooth, but not stretching it.

3. Layer the batting on top and smooth out any wrinkles.

4. Place the quilt top, right side up, on top of the batting. Smooth gently from the center toward the edges until no wrinkles remain.

5. Pin at least every 4" or in each piece of patchwork.

> **tip**
>
> **Basting Larger Quilts**
>
> *For larger quilts, check with local longarm quilters who can provide machine-basting services for a nominal fee.*

QUILTING

Machine Quilting

The best way to quilt on a domestic home machine is to focus on a block or a small section at a time. Use a walking foot when straight stitching and drop the feed dogs when free-motion quilting. Use the needle-down function when stopping and starting to help prevent irregularities in stitching. The more you practice, the better you'll get.

Machine quilting

Hand Quilting

Even if you don't have time to hand quilt an entire quilt, there's no reason you can't combine hand and machine quilting. Always finish the machine quilting first, before beginning any hand quilting or embellishing, to prevent snagging or disturbing the handwork. I often hand quilt big-stitch style with perle cotton #12. The thicker thread and larger stitches allow the texture to show better, and the stitches serve as an accent.

Hand quilting

BINDING

After the quilting is done, trim the excess batting and backing even with the edges of the quilt. Now you're ready to make and apply the binding. I use 2″-wide fabric strips to make double-fold binding on all of my quilts. The yardage amounts given are enough to cut strips up to 2½″ wide if you prefer.

tip

Binding Cleanup
Roll the binding after pressing to keep it tidy.

Make the Binding

1. Cut and sew together the binding strips at a 45° angle as shown. Trim the seams to ¼″ and press them open.

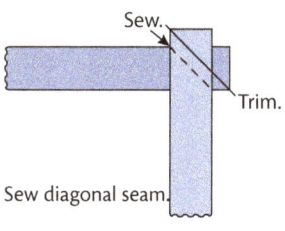
Sew diagonal seam.

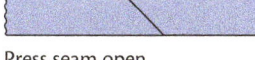
Press seam open.

2. Press the binding in half lengthwise, wrong sides together.

Bind the Quilt

1. With raw edges even, pin the binding to the front edge of the quilt a few inches away from a corner. Begin sewing, leaving the first few inches of the binding unattached and using a ¼″ seam allowance. Stop ¼″ away from the first corner and backstitch one stitch.

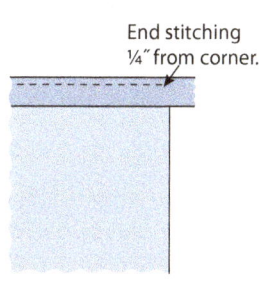
Stitch to ¼″ from corner.

2. Lift the presser foot and raise the needle. Rotate the quilt a quarter turn. Fold the binding at a right angle so it extends straight above the quilt and the fold forms a 45° angle in the corner

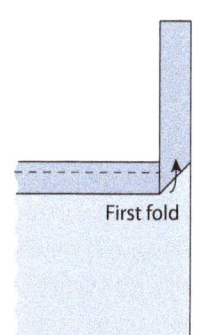
First fold for miter

3. Fold the binding strip down even with the next edge of the quilt. Begin sewing at the folded edge. Continue sewing and repeat in the same manner at all corners.

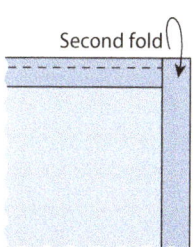
Fold binding down.

Finish the Binding

1. Fold the ending tail of the binding back on itself where it meets the beginning of the binding. From the fold, measure and mark the cut width of your binding strip. Cut the binding tail at this measurement. For example, if your binding is cut 2″ wide, measure 2″ from the fold and cut the binding tail to this length.

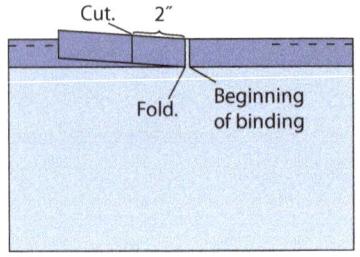

Measure and cut.

2. Unfold both binding tails. Place one end on top of the other at right angles, right sides together. Mark a diagonal line from corner to corner and stitch on the line. Check that you've done it correctly and that the binding fits the quilt; then trim the seam allowance to ¼″. Finger-press the seams open.

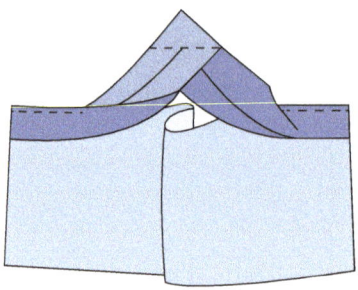

Sew diagonal seam.

3. Refold the binding and stitch the remaining binding in place on the quilt.

4. Press the binding away from the front of the quilt and fold it over the raw edges to the quilt back. Secure with binding clips; hand stitch using a blind hem stitch and a thread color that matches the binding.

MAKE A LABEL

Always add a label to the back of your quilt! Include your name, the quilter's name (if it was quilted by someone else), the date, and the location where the quilt was made. Add other important information, such as the recipient and the special occasion or reason for giving the quilt. You won't always be with your quilt to provide that information, so a label ensures that the information won't get lost.

Have fun with the label by adding elements from the front of the quilt. Or develop your own trademark label by adding a design that is unique to you. Every one of my labels is different because I use scraps from the front of the quilt and either a single block or portion of a block. Often I will choose the color ink to coordinate as well. Computer-printed labels are nice, but your handwriting will add a more personal touch. You worked hard on your quilt—put your name on it!

Label your quilt with style!

> **tips**
>
> **Computer Labels**
>
> *If you prefer to use a computer-printed label—such as those on C&T Publishing's Quilt Label Collective CD, Volumes I, II, and III—make it personal by adding your own lettering and coloring. Print directly onto fabric prepared for an inkjet printer or use a transfer product such as Lesley Riley's TAP Transfer Artist Paper (by C&T Publishing; see Resources, page 111).*

blanks FOR COLORING

Part of the fun of using scraps is figuring out how to make them work for the quilt pattern you want to use. On the following pages, you'll find blank quilt diagrams that you can copy and color to experiment with different color schemes. Remember the SCRAPS secrets and you'll be designing dynamic scrap quilts in no time!

Citrus Squeeze
(quilt photo, page 9)

Detour
(quilt photo, page 56)

Fusion
(quilt photo, page 40)

Homespun Hearts
(quilt photo, page 12)

Oh My Stars
(quilt photo, page 70)

BLANKS FOR COLORING

Paper Chain
(quilt photo, page 48)

Peppermint Pie
(quilt photo, page 80)

Razzmatazz
(quilt photo, page 60)*

* *To allow for larger coloring spaces, this blank quilt diagram has fewer blocks than the pictured quilt (page 60).*

Tipsy Tac Toe
(quilt photo, page 26)

BLANKS FOR COLORING

Zephyr
(quilt photo, page 34)

About the Author

Photo by Kelly Knott

Diane D. Knott was born and raised in southern Louisiana. After graduating from High Point University in North Carolina, she spent almost a decade as a flight attendant for American Airlines. She and her husband, Bill, are raising their three children in northern Georgia.

While growing up, Diane loved sleeping under the beautiful hand-stitched quilts made by her great-grandmother. When Diane was expecting her first child, she enrolled in a quilting class to learn how to make a baby quilt. Almost 20 years and many, many quilts later, she loves quilting for family and friends. Quilts made from the scraps of those quilted gifts are her favorites because there are memories in every stitch!

Diane is a contributing writer for Craftsy.com. Her designs are published in various quilt magazines and calendars on a regular basis. She enjoys sharing her quilts with guilds and groups through trunk shows and workshops. Her teaching and workshop schedule can be found on her website at **butterflythreadsquilting.com**. When she's not quilting, she can be found cheering for her kids at their sporting events, tending her vegetable garden, reading historical fiction, or traveling with her family.

RESOURCES

Fabric and Batting

All solid fabrics used in the quilts in this book are from the American Made Brand, courtesy of Clothworks. To learn more about this line of fabric that is grown, manufactured, and produced exclusively in the USA, and for a list of retail outlets, please visit clothworks.com.

All Kaffe Fassett fabrics used in this book are courtesy of Westminster Fabrics. To find them and many other beautiful prints, and for a list of retail outlets, visit westminsterfabrics.com.

The batting in each quilt is Warm and White, courtesy of the Warm Company. For their complete selection of cotton battings and a list of retail outlets, visit warmcompany.com.

Notions

The following products are available at your local quilt store or at ctpub.com:

- Carol Doak's Foundation Paper
- fast2sew™ Ultimate Seam Guide
- Lesley Riley's TAP Transfer Artist Paper
- *Quilt Label Collective* CD—Volumes I, II, and III

www.ingramcontent.com/pod-product-compliance
Lightning Source LLC
Chambersburg PA
CBHW051551220426
43671CB00025B/2999